REF 03

Warman's®

Kitschy Kitchen

Collectibles

FIELD GUIDE

Brian S. Alexander

Values and Identification

Canon City, Colorado

©2005 KP Books
Published by

kp books
An Imprint of F+W Publications

700 East State Street • Iola, WI 54990-0001
715-445-2214 • 888-457-2873

Our toll-free number to place an order or obtain
a free catalog is (800) 258-0929.

Materials excerpted from *Spiffy Kitchen Collectibles* © 2003
Brian S. Alexander, used with permission.

Library of Congress Catalog Number: 2005924816
ISBN: 0-89689-251-4

Designed by Kay Sanders
Edited by Tracy L. Schmidt

Printed in China

Acknowledgments

The generous support of the following people made this book possible: Carol Alexander, who was there from the first page, thanks mom! My fabulous brothers and sisters, Jody, Greg, Doug, Diane, Shirley, Kent, and Jay—and my niece Dawn, thanks for being there for this one and the others. Eric Zorn and fellow members of his SIN support group, author Walter Oleksy and members in his writer's group, Paul Kennedy and Tracy Schmidt at KP Books. Bindy Bitterman at Eureka! Antiques, Evanston, IL, for assistance with proofreading and a few wonderful finds! Patricia McDaniel at Storefront Antiques, Dublin, IN; Angie Wegner at Hawthorn Antique Mall & Gallery, Bristol, WI; and Marsha Brandom, cyber friend and supporter. Many of these people were there in the gray days of the project, where a change in the weather could (and sometimes did) affect the outcome.

Others helpful were John Leonard, Michelle Rioli, Tony Iuro, Matt Haylock, Robert Katzman at Magazine Memories, The Antique Market in Michigan City, IN; The Broadway Antique Market in Chicago; Douglas, Tim, Andy, and Tina. Assistance also came from Abbott Labs APCRU unit in Waukegan and their friendly staff, Osco film in Michigan City, Kinko's copies, U. S. Postal Service, the hundreds of Ebay sellers around the country (and world!).

A final thanks must be given to all those procrastinating cooks out there who never quite got around to using that what-cha-ma-callit!

CONTENTS

Contents

Additionally I want to express my thanks to the many antiques malls, shops and shows tapped to assemble the items pictured in these pages, their locales follow. **Illinois:** Chicago, Wilmette, Gurnee, Volo, St. Charles, Rockford, Richmond, Hebron, Springfield, Wilmington, Des Plaines, Princeton, Sandwich, Grayslake. **Wisconsin :** Milwaukee, Racine, Kenosha, Bristol, Lake Geneva, Milton, Madison, Mount Horeb. **Indiana:** LaPorte, Chesterton, Valparaiso, Pines, Michigan City, Crown Point, South Bend, Pierceton, Lafayette, Delphi, Peru, Rochester, Boswell, Kentland, Fairmount, Lebanon, Indianapolis, Portland, Knightstown, Dublin, Richmond. **Michigan:** Niles, Lakeside, Union Pier, Sawyer, Allegan, Bangor. **Ohio:** Springfield, Dayton, and Columbus. **Iowa:** Des Moines.

Introduction

I'm happy to present the numerous objects shown in *Kitchy Kitchen Collectibles* for your interest, amusement, and perhaps wonderment. Throughout the book, numerous period magazines, advertisements, and related materials are shown to help relate the objects pictured to the approximate era when they were produced. In many cases, these showcase the 'bright modern outlook' theme so prevalent in advertising images and product designs from the late 1940s to the 1960s. These optimistic images seem to convey the thought that yes, your life, or at least the chore at hand, could be better, easier, and faster if you would only use the product shown and not some lesser item available elsewhere.

All the items pictured are from my collection except as noted, and represent a broad spectrum of kitchen items and cooking activities. These include just about every task you would want to try to master in your kitchen of yesteryear. There are gadgets of all types, some of which question the intelligence of the user by their lack of necessity, and all sorts of accessories, sets, holders, and miscellaneous gizmos. Most of the items are non-electrical and small in scale; however, a few electrical and bigger items managed to find their way in as well.

The book tries to present examples that best show the various categories along with corresponding printed materials that help to explain how the products were used. Although only a fraction of the possible items that might fit the scope of the book are shown, the examples pictured help tell the story or history, if you will, of a time when elaborate meal preparation was a daily activity and convenience and prepackaged foods weren't so readily available.

Today, when big box stores have begun to transform the retail landscape, this book helps turn back the hands of that colorful kitchen clock to a not so distant past. It recalls a time when you could roam the aisles of your local store and perhaps find that special something you just couldn't do without (hopefully like this book). Happy Hunting!

Brian S. Alexander

Brian S. Alexander

Collecting Kitchenware/ Household Objects

The diverse area of kitchenware/household objects offers a world of collecting opportunities. Your interests may lead you to antique rarities more than one-hundred-years old or to items of more recent manufacture. Any and all territory should be considered fair game. As with other collectibles, your primary motivation should be your individual likes and preferences.

One question beginning collectors should ask, is how specialized they want their collections to be. Setting limits for your collecting range or territory is an important factor. You may be interested in true antiques for a display or you may want to concentrate on certain items such as molds, and have multiple examples that span a longer time period. Occasionally you will hear about a particularly interesting kitchenware/household object such as a heart-shaped ice-cream scoop from the 1920s, or an 1880s swan-shaped iron bringing thousands of dollars at auction. Many collectors marvel at these rarities, but can find a world of satisfaction collecting items in lower price ranges.

At the present time, there is a great deal of interest in kitchenware and related items from 35 to 60 years old; these objects rekindle old memories and represent a different, less-complicated era for many. As with other collectibles, this increased interest has created an upward curve in prices. Items that could be bought for a few dollars ten years ago are now generally worth five to ten times that amount, and higher-priced items have increased almost as much. This increase in interest has created opportunities for the informed collector. Some sellers may not recognize a utilitarian kitchenware object as being particularly valuable, or their interests may lie elsewhere. That's why the gizmo grandma had in her cupboard for decades might go for a fraction of its worth to an interested collector. But as a result of Internet auctions, many sellers are more informed and these types of bargains are harder to find.

Another factor affecting kitchenware items is the scarcity factor, as it relates to value. Few items from the last 50 years or so can be considered unique or one of a kind. However, it may happen that a certain vintage item, unused and in mint condition with its original label intact, and perhaps its original carton and price tag from the local store, becomes such a curiosity that its rarity and appeal to collectors is greatly enhanced. This can add appreciably to the item's value and price. If only one out of one hundred of these items still exists in this as-new condition, the scarcity curve is increased and the object, even if it was widely available when new, can now be considered scarce.

Collectors should let their interests guide them. If an object in mint as-new condition sufficiently adds to its worth to them, they can justify the added cost. In general, a vintage object that is mint and has its original graphically interesting box or packaging is worth about 25% more than a similar, nicely used example without its box.

Internet auctions have provided a way to discover more of these rarities and make them available for purchase. There are times when an object on screen becomes overwhelmingly irresistible to a collector. A word I made up to describe this appeal is Ebacious, a corny combination of Ebay and delicious. You know you've experienced an Ebacious object when you can't get it out of your mind, and your primary thoughts are focused on when the auction is scheduled to be over and what strategy might best ensure that you're the winning bidder. However, if someone else also finds the same object irresistible, the price of the item can easily escalate to unreasonable levels. Can you justify a hefty price tag for an item which might ordinarily sell for much less at a local antique mall or show? If so, proceed with caution, because it's likely a chance to acquire a similar object at a much lower price will come up, if you just exercise a little patience.

Another way a patient collector can acquire items at reasonable cost is to buy an object with a missing or broken part, usually at a considerable discount. In many instances the missing or broken piece can be replaced with an identical one, and the object becomes more valuable than the total cost you paid for it.

As with other collecting endeavors, in kitchenware it's foremost that the collector be happy with their collection. If an added benefit of collecting is the increase in value, fine, but potential value increases shouldn't drive your collecting. Another benefit for kitchen collectors is that many of the objects can still be used and function as well as, or better than, new items of the same type. With thorough cleaning and care, the object will retain its value and be an asset to your household rather than just a hands-off museum piece.

The World of Gadgets and How We Got There

A clear definition of what constitutes a gadget is somewhat elusive. According to a 1940s *Life Magazine* article, a gadget is a, "device for doing something that nobody knew needed doing until a gadget was invented to do it!" Although there may be some truth to this notion, the present day use of the word gadget has evolved through the years to encompass a broad array of items, mostly hand held, that help to perform a task.

In its broadest sense, even the simplest item such as a straight pin or a spoon could be described as a gadget. Familiarity with the item makes one forget that there was a time when even a spoon was a novel development needing training or repeated use to gain acceptance. In antiquity, a simple household spoon or knife was a prized possession, with the use of a fork for eating a relatively recent development stemming from France in the mid-eighteenth century. By the 1800s, knife, spoon, and fork utensil sets for eating became commonplace. This set the stage for the adoption of servers and other utensils.

In view of this history one might ask, how did the catchall gadget category as we know it today evolve? The first gadgets got their start in the era of Yankee ingenuity. In 1875, D.

Top Value Stamp Catalog. Cover picture shows a typically well-dressed family doing some window-shopping, mid-1950s. **$15-$18**

H. Goodell started a firm to make apple peelers and other devices out of cast iron. This company continued into the modern era with its core business intact. Others followed, including importers of overseas kitchen specialties such as Gustav Thurnauer. These businesses flourished on the East Coast where more distributors became involved and started selling similar items made at local sources. One of these source companies was the A&J Co. of Binghampton, N.Y., that made kitchen utensils and egg beaters. This created the manufacturing and distribution network that led the gadget and housewares industries into the twentieth century.

By the 1920s, gadgets had emerged as a distinct classification of housewares. In these earlier days of merchandising, it was common for stores to stash away smaller utilitarian items in drawers, limiting their access to customers. In the 1930s, an innovative east coast merchandiser, Michael Barry, and his family started selling gadget type items in bins along with illustrative placards that showed how they were to be used. This sales strategy helped invigorate the entire category by attracting the customer's attention and boosting sales. As more stores adopted this strategy, a separate sales area for gadgets became commonplace, giving the category a higher profile to customers and manufacturers. Along with this trend, the use of the word gadget evolved as a familiar way to describe these items.

In the 1940s, manufacturers began routinely mounting gadget-type devices on separate illustrative cards that could be wall or rack hung. The early versions of these used simple graphics and were somewhat utilitarian in appearance. This evolved by the 1950s into colorful pictures and graphics to help attract and hold the customer's attention. Sometimes the packaging used on these items seems more interesting than the objects themselves! Today, collectors look at a common kitchen gadget still attached to its original sales card or packaging as a seldom seen survivor, adding history, interest, curiosity, and in most cases a substantial increase in value.

Metal Canister Set, decorative kitchen gadget design, marked Weibro/Chicago. A matching wastebasket was also available, 1950s-1960s. **$40-$45**

Goodell White Mountain Apple Parer, Corer, and Slicer, Goodell Co., Antrim, NH. 1950s. **$40-$45**

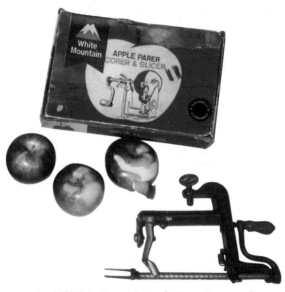

Goodell White Mountain Apple Parer, Corer, and Slicer, Goodell Co., Antrim, NH, 1960s. **$30-$35**

Flaming Snowballs Advertising Box, Heilemann Ice Cream, Jefferson, WI. Coconut-covered ice-cream balls were a festive accessory for that elegant 1950s-1960s dinner party. **$10-$12**

Aluminum Measuring Spoon Set, accurate, handy, four sizes on card, 1940s. **$15-$18**

Mendets. "Mends all leaks instantly, simply tighten. Don't throw it away, mend it with mendets," on card, 1940s, U S Standard. **$12-$15**

Cherry Pitter, metal, "For fresh and preserved fruit, Knocks out the pits," on card, 1940s, Kenberry, J.C.Brown Inc., Belleville, NJ. **$8-$10**

New Meco Fiz-Kap, "Keeps the pep in your beverages," on card, 1940s, Collette Mfg. Co, Amsterdam, NY. **$12-$15**

Chef's Triple Vegetable Cutter, metal, "Cut large and small strips," with insert card, 1940s, M&M Kitchen Aids, Chicago, IL. **$15-$18**

Strawberry Huller & Pinfeather Picker, "Serves ice cubes, radishes, pickles, etc.," on card, 1941. **$8-$10**

Household Specialties Co., Union, NJ, French Fry Cutter and Garnishing Knife, stainless-steel blade with wood handle, on card, 1940s. **$15-$18**

Spee Dee Chopper, on card, 1950s, Kenberry, J.C. Brown, Inc., Belleville, NJ. **$10-$12**

Kitchen Saw, "Cuts the hardest bones, a wonderful kitchen tool," on card, 1950, Kenberry, J.C. Brown, Inc., Belleville, NJ. **$12-$15**

Cookie & Pastry Tool, on card, 1956, Kenberry, J.C. Brown, Inc., Belleville, NJ. **$10-$12**

Saturday Evening Post, February 26, 1955, with cover illustration by Stevan Dohanos. The ladies are at a bridal shower admiring an eggbeater and other mid-fifties treasures. **$8-$10**

Punch-n-Cover, metal spike punches hole in evaporated milk can and acts as a cover, on card, 1950s, Mueller Mfg. Co., Greenville, MS. **$12-$15**

Hostess Gadgets, for the kitchen, five different tools, serving tongs, wire slicer, jar wrench, strawberry huller, and ejector fork, on card, 1930s, Kenberry, J.C. Brown, Inc., Belleville, NJ. **$22-$25**

Em-Ree Jar Lifter, metal, "To lift any hot, cold, open, or closed jar with safety," boxed 1940s, Emery & Sons Co., Detroit, MI. **$18-$22**

Vapor-Vacuum Seal Opener, metal, "A quick easy way to open glass jars," on card, 1940s, White Cap Co., Chicago IL. **$12-$15**

Acme Rotary Mincer, stainless steel blade with wood handle, "For mincing, cutting noodles, etc.," in red or green with instructions, boxed, 1935. **$22- $25**

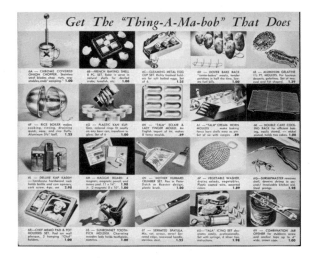

Get The "Thing-A-Ma-bob" That Does

6A — CHROME COVERED ONION CHOPPER. Stainless steel blades chop nuts, vegetables, ends" escaping. **1.00**

6B —FRENCH BAKING SHELL 8 PC. SET. Bake to serve in natural shells for deviled crabs, turnfish, etc. **1.00**

6C—GLEAMING METAL EGG CUP SET. Richly finished holders for soft boiled eggs. Set of 6. **1.25**

6D — DOVER BAKE RACK "center-bakes" mealy, tender potatoes in half the time, lowers fuel bills. **1.00**

6E — ALUMINUM GELATINE 1½ PT. MOULDS. For luscious desserts, gelatines. Set of two oval and fish shaped. **1.39**

6F — RICE BOILER makes cooking, rinsing, draining quick, easy, and rice fluffy. Aluminum 3½" bolt. **1.35**

6G — PLASTIC KAN KLIP. Gray, colored rings fit neatly on any beer can, transform to glass. Set of 6. **1.00**

6H — "TALA" ECLAIR & LADY FINGER MOULD. An English import of tin, makes 8 fancy moulds. **.69**

6I — "TALA" CREAM HORN MOULDS make baking fancy horn shells easy as pie. Set of six with recipes. **.69**

6K — DOUBLE CAKE COOL-ING RACK for efficient baking, easily stored, — nickel plated, holds two cakes. **1.00**

6L — DELUXE KAP KADDY — handsome hardwood rack holds bottle and can openers, cork screw. 4 pc. set **2.98**

6M — MAGGIE BOARD. 4 magnets, magnetic pencil, and memo pad. 11 x 14". **1.95** Jr. (2 magnets) 8 x 10". **1.00**

6N — MOTHER HUBBARD CRUMBER SET. Pan in Penn-Dutch or Rooster design, plastic brush. **1.00**

6P — VEGETABLE WASHER. drains salads, vegetables. Plastic coated wire, assorted colors. **1.89**

6Q—SHRIMPMASTER removes shell, deveins shrimp in seconds! Invaluable kitchen aid. Steel prongs. **1.98**

6R—CHEF MEMO PAD & POT HOLDERS SET. Pad on wall plaque, 2 hanging "Chef" holders. **1.00**

6S — SUNBONNET TOOTH-PICK HOLDER. Charming wooden lady holds toothpicks, matches. **1.00**

6T — SERRATED SPATULA. Mix, cut, scrape, serve! Serrated edge, rosewood handle, stainless steel. **1.35**

6U—"TALA" ICING SET decorates easily, professionally. Set with syringe, 6 silver tips, instructions. **1.98**

6V — COMBINATION JAR OPENER for stubborn screw and anchor tops up to 4" wide, crown caps. **1.00**

Housewares Catalog. (left and right) Pages from Robertson's of South Bend, IN, mid-1950s. Note the variety and quality of items available for about $1. A number of these are shown in other sections of this book. Value of entire catalog: **$12-$15**

House Furnishings Review published this photo of a typical gadget bar inside a hardware store in the late 1940s—early 1950s.

House Furnishings Review contained this picture of Michael Barry and his New York Gadget Shop in the early 1930s.

According to the original caption for this picture appearing in *House Furnishings Review,* "farming people are more gadget conscious than city folks," as they stand before an early 1950s gadget bar.

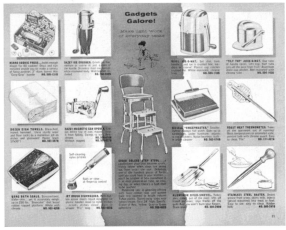

Housewares catalog page from the *Acehi Stamp Catalog*, mid 1950s. **$12-$15**

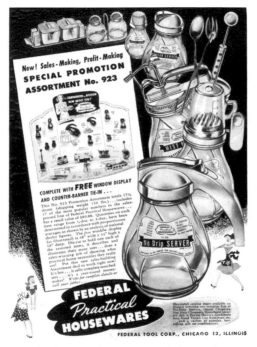

Federal Practical Housewares ad showing their 1940s product line and a store window display, *House Furnishing Review*, July 10, 1948. **$2-$5**

Catalog pages from the *Holden Trading Stamp Catalog*, mid-1950s. **$12-$15**

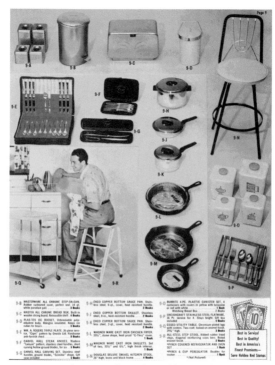

Catalog pages from the *Holden Trading Stamp Catalog*, mid-1950s. **$12-$15**

Colorful Decals having a kitchen or gadget theme make a fun addition to kitchen collections.

Meyercord Decals with collages of kitchen items, "For a colorful home," 1940s-1950s. **$10-$12**

Chapter 1

Barbecue Tools, Aprons, Accessories and Miscellaneous

Barbecue items helped promote the all American activity of the backyard cookout. These products produced in the 1950s for a growing suburban marketplace usually have a whimsical or humorous viewpoint. At most cookouts, the chef played a center-stage role. It was only natural that he or she should wear an entertaining or humorous smock to help enliven the activities. Other products such as tool sets, and barbecue accessories had a similar impact, adding to their appeal. Collectors today look for unusual or interesting items with fanciful designs that help recall the 1950s era.

Androck Steak Broiler, metal, "For outdoor appetites," with insert card, 1950s, The Washburn Co. **$12-$15**

Everywoman's Magazine, July 1955. Here's a great scene of pre-cookout preparation 1950s style. The admiring looks could be due to the chef's first prize ribbon, although not for this meal, it hasn't been cooked yet! **$6-$8**

Shish Kabab, aluminum rotating grill attachment, boxed, 1950s, Wil-Nor Products, Tarzana, CA. **$15-$18**

Clyde Bar-B-Q Set, deluxe three-piece stainless steel set with wooden handles, boxed, 1950s, Clyde Cutlery Co., Clyde, OH. **$20-$22**

Longhorn Meat Markers, 12 metal cooking level markers, boxed, 1950s, Bar & Barbecue Products, Los Angeles, CA. **$15-$18**

Bar-B-Q Tumble Basket, "For the best in greaseless outdoor charcoal cooking," with insert card 1950s. **$18-$22**

Picnic or Barbecue, as shown in a 1950s
Top Value Stamps Catalog. **$12-$15**

Barbecue Set, five pieces, chrome plated with wooden handles, boxed, 1950s. **$25-$35**

Skotch O' matic Hot or Cold Jug, metal and plastic, 1/2 gal, "Press the bulb, it serves a drink, a delight to use!," boxed, 1950s, Hamilton- Skotch Corp., Hamilton, OH. **$30-$35**

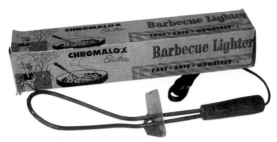

Chromalox Electric Barbecue Lighter, "Fast, safe, odorless," boxed, 1950s, Chromalox, Murfreesboro, TN. **$15-$18**

Skotch Ice, cans of freezable liquid were reusable ice cubes, "Keeps food and drink cold, the dry way—no messy melting," in package, 1950s, Hamilton-Skotch Corp. **$18-$22**

Skotch Picnic Kooler, insulated metal with lid and plastic tray for dry foods, 1950s, Hamilton-Skotch Corp. **$22-$25**

Spiffy Jug, insulated metal with plastic lid, was also made in green & blue, 1950s, Hamilton-Skotch Corp. **$22-$25**

Arthur Godfrey Barbecue, with charcoal inside, "The charcoal pit for broiling your food," with cardboard insert, 1950s, Marc Mfg. Co., Chicago, IL. **$28-$35**

Barbecue Tool Set, stainless steel with "No-slip safety handles, For the outdoor chef," boxed, 1950s, Washington Forge. **$25-$35**

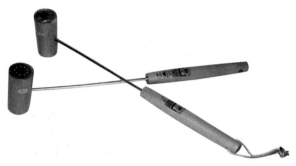

Androck Barbecue Salt & Pepper Shakers, stainless steel and wood with leather hangers, 1950s, The Washburn Co., Worcester MA and Rockford, IL. **$15-$18**

Instant Charcoal Grill, "No lighter fluid needed, take anywhere," 1950s-1960s, E-Z-Por Corp., "Products for better living," Chicago, IL. **$15-$18**

Sweet Apple-Wood Smoke Flakes, 1950s, Patrick Cudahy Inc., Cudahy, WI. **$12-$15**

Tuck, "Durable heavy plastic tablecloth, for parties and picnics," boxed, 1950s, Technical Tape Corp., New Rochelle, NY. **$8-$10**

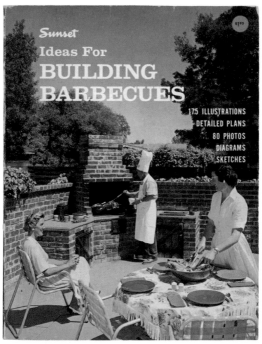

Sunset *Ideas for Building Barbecues,* 1950s-1960s.
These folks are having a relaxed, rather proper barbecue,
notice the lack of a comical design on the apron. **$8-$10**

Toas-Tite, metal with wood handles, "Makes a delicious sealed in drip proof hot toasted sandwich," boxed, 1950s, Bar-B-Buns, Inc., Cincinnati, OH. **$18-$22**

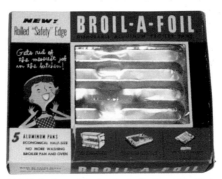

Broil-A-Foil, disposable aluminum broiler pans, "Gets rid of the messiest job in the kitchen," boxed, 1950s-1960s, Metal Foil Products Mfg. Co., Linden, NJ. **$8-$10**

Swift's Premium ad with Sandwich Toaster offer, from *Family Circle*, June 1950. **$2-$5**

Sandwich Toasters were a 1950s gadget that allowed you to put bread, meat, cheese, etc. into a hinged metal cooking unit and toast the contents over a stove or campfire.

Snack Toaster, metal with wood handles, "Toasted sealed sandwiches, America's new taste delight," boxed, 1950s, Federal Mfg. & Engr. Corp., Brooklyn, NY. **$18-$22**

Kloth Klips, set of four metal tablecloth clips, "For gracious outdoor living," Acme Metal Goods Mfg. Co., Newark, NJ. This example was found in an antiques store in Peru, IN. **$12-$15**

Gadget Master Hot Vegetable Tongs, metal, "No more burned fingers, A star in any kitchen," boxed, 1950s, Popiel Bros, Chicago, IL. **$18-$22**

Hi-Speed Safety Kitchen Tongs, metal, "For hot vegetables and other uses, prevents burned fingers," boxed, 1940s, Kitchen Gadget Mfg. Co., Asbury Park, NJ. **$18-$20**

Oven Shovel, metal, 'The safe, sane way to handle hot pies, cakes, dishes, etc.," boxed, 1950s, Dor-File Mfg. Co., Portland, OR. **$18-$20**

Non-Splash Spatula, stainless steel, "The safe way of turning food in frying pan or griddle," boxed, 1950s, Buckly Culinary Products, Chicago, IL. **$18-$20**

Surface Cooker, "For even-heat cooking on any top-of-the-stove burner, Makes food taste better," in package, 1950s, Arthur Beck Corp., Chicago, IL. **$18-$22**

Bake King Burner Chef Heat Diffuser, metal with wood handle, "Makes a double boiler of every pan in your kitchen," in package, 1950s, Chicago Metallic Mfg. Co., Chicago, IL, Artbeck. **$18-$22**

Chapter 2

Basters, Roasting Accessories, Potato Bakers, Etc.

The baster, according to Julia Child in the *Art of French Cooking*, was one of America's great culinary contributions. Its acceptance by cooks is apparent by the numerous varieties produced over the years. Today, the baster is one of a number of roasting accessories gaining acceptance by collectors. These include skewers, heat rods, slicing aids, and other helpers. Examples including a colorful original box or container are most sought after by collectors.

A number of vintage products were produced to promote the ease and speed of potato baking. Potato nails were commonly seen gadgets. These metal spikes helped speed up the cooking process through faster heat conduction. Examples on their original packaging card make fun collection additions.

1958 Standard Oil Calendar, from W. Lafayette, Indiana. Crisis in the kitchen, 1950s style, the young lady shown is sobbing when her turkey won't fit in the oven and her husband is pondering their options. **$22-$25**

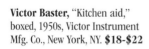

Ohio Baster, for roast meat and fowl, in cardboard tube, 1950s, Ohio Thermometer Co., Springfield, OH. **$18-$22**

Victor Baster, "Kitchen aid," boxed, 1950s, Victor Instrument Mfg. Co., New York, NY. **$18-$22**

Ideal Baster, heat proof, "The wonder kitchen utensil," boxed, 1950s, Victor Instrument Mfg. Co., New York, NY. **$18-$22**

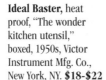

Ade-O-Matic, internal and external baster, unbreakable stainless steel, in cardboard tube, 1950s, Ade-O-Matic Co., Chicago, IL. **$18-$22**

Turkey Lacers, rustproof, "stuffing is easy," on card, 1950s, The Harwood Co., Farmingdale, NJ. **$10-$12**

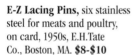

E-Z Lacing Pins, six stainless steel for meats and poultry, on card, 1950s, E.H.Tate Co., Boston, MA. **$8-$10**

No Sew Turkey Lacer, stainless steel, "Easy, Quick, Sanitary," on card, 1950s, M.E. Heuck Co., Cincinnati, OH. **$8-$10**

Stuffin' Plate, copper-tone aluminum, "No strings, needles, skewers," on card, 1950s, Color Craft, Indianapolis, IN. **$12-$15**

Baking Nails, six jumbo size, aluminum, "Bake potatoes tastier and faster," on card, 1950s-1960s, Wecolite Co., Teaneck, NJ. **$10-$12**

Roasting Pan, metal, "Easy to clean, Completely seamless, Surehold handles," with label, 1950s, Bake King, Chicago Metallic Mfg. Co., Lake Zurich, IL. **$18-$20**

Foley Roaster, Teflon-finished metal, "With adjustable 'V' rack for full heat circulation," boxed, 1960s, Foley Mfg. Co., Mnpls, MN. **$15-$18**

Ekco Diathermic Cook Rods, aluminum, "For roasts, chicken, ham, etc., A new idea in cooking, saves 25% of cooking time," boxed, 1950s, Ekco Products Co., Chicago, IL. **$18-$22**

Roastand, metal, for oven and grill, "Roasts evenly throughout by scientific method," boxed, 1950s, Domestic Enterprises, Chicago, IL. **$15-$18**

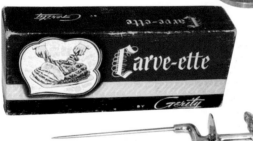

Carve-ette by Gerity, chromed metal, boxed, 1950s, Gerity-Michigan Corp., Adrian, MI. **$15-$18**

See you at my Tupperware Party!

...just a
reminder of
the day.............
the date.............
the time............
and the place...

hostess.............................

TUPPERWARE®
... sold only on the home party plan   THP 944-A   Printed in U.S.A.

"See you at my Tupperware party!" This postcard was used
as a reminder card for an upcoming party, the lady shown
is setting up shop with a Roast Flavor Saver, 1967. **$8-$10**

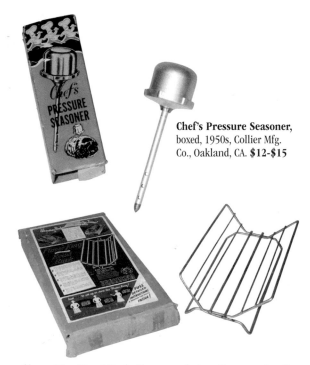

Chef's Pressure Seasoner, boxed, 1950s, Collier Mfg. Co., Oakland, CA. **$12-$15**

Flavor King Roast Rack, "Assures perfect roasting every time," boxed, 1949, Household Necessities, Chicago, IL. **$10-$12**

Baking Nails, six, aluminum, "Cooks from inside out, Cuts cooking time 1/3," on card, 1950s-1960s, M.E. Heuck Co., Cincinnati, OH. **$10-$12**

Spud Spikes, set of six, aluminum, "Exclusive knife edge, Bake potatoes fast," with card sleeve, 1950s, Monarch Die Casting, Santa Monica, CA. **$18-$20**

"Handi Hostess" Potato Basket and Noodle Nest, "Makes a delicious potato basket for parties, luncheons," boxed, 1951, Bonley Products Co., Chicago, IL. **$18-$22**

Bake-Rite Potato Bakers, aluminum, "Bakes potatoes evenly in half the time," on card, 1950s, Kewanee rite Products, Kewanee, IL. **$10-$12**

Dover, "Potatoe-bake" Rack, "Newest, neatest way to bake potatoes," with insert sheet, 1950s, Dover Products Co., Chicago, IL. **$15-$18**

Rembrandt Automatic Potato Peeler, plastic with faucet attachment, "Washes and peels automatically, No work, No waste, and unit cleans itself," boxed, 1950s, All Channel Products Corp., Woodside, NY. **$22-$25**

Potato Bake Rods, set of four "Thermo-kook" aluminum, "Quick baked potatoes, Fast meat roasting," in package, 1959, A Kenberry Product, John Clark Brown Inc., Belleville, NJ. **$12-$15**

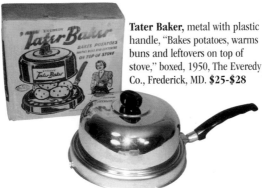

Tater Baker, metal with plastic handle, "Bakes potatoes, warms buns and leftovers on top of stove," boxed, 1950, The Everedy Co., Frederick, MD. **$25-$28**

Chapter 3

Beaters, Mixers, Whippers

Beaters are used to whip cream, eggs, batter, etc. and generally fall into three broad categories: fixed, mechanical, or rotary. Fixed beaters are guided by hand motion and include simple wire and coiled wire designs. Mechanical beaters involve pushing up and down on the top to create a revolving motion. Rotary beaters involve a geared wheel and crank mechanism where rotating blades create the mixing action. Rotary whippers usually have a faster motion that adds additional aeration to the mixture. Beater design has evolved from early primitive examples to modern-era stainless steel and plastic versions. With the number and variety of beaters made over the years, collectors are assured of finding a wide range of items to interest them.

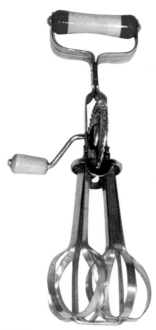

Eggbeater, natural and red wooden handle, "Another Androck Product," 1940s-1950s. **$22-$25**

Eggbeater, stainless steel, cast-metal gear, brown wooden handle, Maid of Honor, 1950s. **$15-$18**

Saturday Evening Post, April 13, 1946, cover illustration by
Constantin Alajalov. It looks like the gentleman shown fell behind
in his party preparations and some guests have joined him in the
kitchen, but they don't seem to be having a good time. **$8-$10**

Eggbeater, A&J high speed, green wooden handle, Ekco Products Co., 1940s-1950s. **$15-$18**

Eggbeater, metal with adjustable top handle, 1940s-1950s, Dazey Mfg. Co., St. Louis, MO. **$20-$25**

Eggbeater, with green Bakelite side handle, 1940s, Worlbeater, Los Angeles, CA. **$30-$35**

Eggbeater, with yellow Bakelite handle, 1940s A&J High Speed, Ekco Products Co. **$20-$22**

Artbeck Whip Beater, with plastic knob, "Whips, beats, mixes, one hand operation," with tube carton, 1954, Arthur Beck Co., Chicago, IL. **$15-$18**

Eggbeater, cast-metal components, black plastic handle, 1950s, Rival Mfg. Co., St. Louis, MO. **$20-$22**

Whip Beater, red and white plastic knob, unmarked, 1950s. **$10-$12**

Mix Matic Food Mixer, "Mixes, beats, whips, blends," boxed, 1950s-1960s, E-Z-Por Corp., Chicago, IL. **$22-$25**

Speed Mixer, stainless steel and plastic with enclosed housing, "Designed for cleanliness," boxed, 1950s, Maynard Mfg. Co., Glendale, CA. **$35-$40**

Artbeck Whip Beater,
wooden knob, with tube
carton, 1948. **$20-$22**

Eggbeater, cast-metal components, turquoise plastic handle, Maynard Mfg. Co., Glendale, CA 1950s-1960s. **$15-$18**

Maynard Speed Mixer ad from *House Furnishing Review,* November 1951.

Blue Whirl Beater ad
from *House Furnishing Review*, May 1951.

Blue Whirl Eggbeater, stainless-steel blades, plastic handle,
1950s, The Turner & Seymour Co., Torrington, NC. **$18-$22**

Dazey Mix-er-ator, with graduations and mixing directions, 1950s, Dazey Corp., St. Louis, MO. **$20-$25**

Whixit Mixer, with graduations, 1950s, Taylor Churn Co, St. Louis, MO. **$18-$20**

Jiffywhip Whipper, "Whips any quantity eggs, batters, cream," boxed, 1940s-1950s, R Krasberg & Sons, Chicago, IL. **$25-$28**

Speed-E-Whipper, "It's amazing, beats, blends, whips, mixes, and many other uses you yourself will discover," yellow with embossed glass, 1950s. **$18-$22** Red with printed glass, boxed, 1950s. **$25-$28**

Minit Cream Whip, "The Wonder," green wooden handle, boxed, 1930s-1940s, D-M Mfg. Co., Detroit, MI. **$35-$40**

Duplex Whipper, metal with green wood handle, "Double action for cream, eggs, and dressings," boxed, 1930s-1940s. **$40-$45**

A&J/Ekco Whippit, "Whips cream in an instant," boxed,
1930s-1940s, Ekco Products Co., Chicago, IL. **$35-$40**

Whippit, cream and egg whip, "They all say whip it with whippit–more than 500,000 users," marbled green wooden handle, boxed, 1930s-1940s, Indestro Mfg. Co., Chicago, IL. **$40-$45**

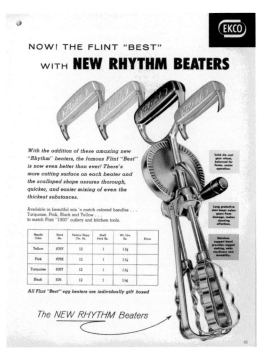

NOW! THE FLINT "BEST"

WITH **NEW RHYTHM BEATERS**

With the addition of these amazing new "Rhythm" beaters, the famous Flint "Best" is now even better than ever! There's more cutting surface on each beater and the scalloped shape assures thorough, quicker, and easier mixing of even the thickest substances.

Available in beautiful mix 'n match colored handles . . . Turquoise, Pink, Black and Yellow . . . to match Flint "1900" cutlery and kitchen tools.

Handle Color	Stock No.	Factory Ship. Ctn. Ea.	Shelf Pack Ea.	Wt. Lbs. Ea.	Price
Yellow	676Y	12	1	1¼	
Pink	676X	12	1	1¼	
Turquoise	676T	12	1	1¼	
Black	676	12	1	1¼	

All Flint "Best" egg beaters are individually gift boxed

The NEW RHYTHM Beaters

Solid die cast gear wheel, balanced for faster, easier operation.

Long protective skirt keeps nylon gears from damage, makes cleaning effortless.

Stainless support band provides rugged staking, adds sturdiness and durability.

Ekco/Flint Rhythm Beaters from an Ekco Products catalog. This was Ekco's top-of-the-line beater in 1957, the new wavy design blades, "made their best even better!"

Ekco Egg Beaters, Flint Rhythm Beaters, lightly used in turquoise, yellow or pink. **$18-$25**

Ekco Rhythm Beater, black plastic handle, boxed, 1950s. **$22-$25**

Eggbeater, Flint, with rhythm beaters, coordinates with flint stainless steel utensils, 1950s. **$15-$22**

Ekco Egg Beater, black with spade handle, stainless steel blades and original insert card, Ekco/A&J, 1950s. **$22-$25**

Ekco Egg Beater, red with white stripes, flared "T" handle with high-speed center drive, Ekco/USA, 1950s. **$18-$25**

Ekco Egg Beater, yellow and white with spade handle and high-speed center drive, Ekco/A&J 1950s. **$18-$25**

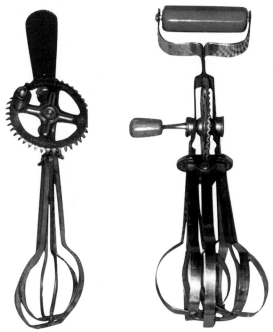

A&J Egg Beaters, with 1923 patent date, this model was made at A&J prior to being acquired by Ekco in 1929. Examples with little paint loss or other signs of wear command top prices: Red handle, Ekco/A&J Egg Beater. **$22-$25** Green handle, 1930s. **$18-$22**

Egg Beaters from a 1957 Ekco Products catalog. Over the years eggbeaters were made in a variety of styles and price ranges. Versions with eight stainless steel blades were considered a step up from plated eight or four-blade models.

Chapter 4

Cake and Mold Pans

Vintage cake and mold pans come in a variety of shapes and sizes. Many pans were created to help celebrate holidays, birthdays, and other events. The pan shape sometimes helps determine the event to be celebrated such as a heart for Valentine's Day or a tree or star for Christmas. Most pans from the 1930s to 1960s originally were sold with colorful, graphically interesting labels or packaging. These materials usually provided information on product use and suggested recipes. It's not common to find a vintage pan with its original label, since use of the product usually meant removing the label. However, some labels were saved over the years for their recipes. Expect to pay a 35% or higher premium for a vintage pan still retaining its original label. Cake and mold pans having a figural shape or including the design of a well-known, licensed character usually have increased collector value.

Spring Form Cake Pan, "For sponge cake, sunshine cake, fruit cake, etc.," with label, 1950s, Ekco Products Co./Ovenex. **$25-$28**

Swans Down Cake Pan, "Swans Down cake flour makes better cakes," 1920s. **$25-$30**

Swans Down Cake Pan, (side view), Pat. Dec 18-23, 1920s, E. Katzinger Co. **$25-$30**

Upside Down Cake Pan with label, 1950s, Ekco Products Co./Ovenex. **$25-$28**

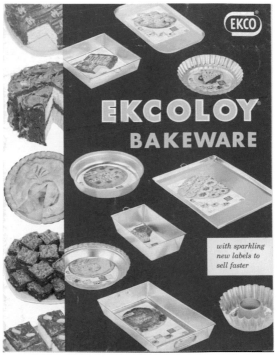

Ekcolay Bakeware product catalog, "women prefer Ekcolay 2 to 1," 1950s. Catalog value: **$15-$18**

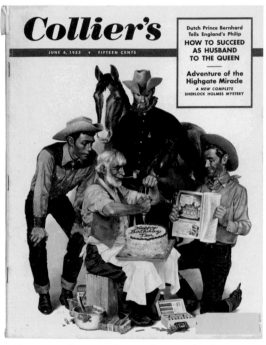

Collier's, June 6, 1953, with cover illustration by Glenn
Grohe. Unusual cake decorating scene shows cowboys trying
to recreate a luscious cake from a magazine ad. **$8-$10**

Kate Smith's Bake-a-Cake Kit, with two pans, recipe booklets, and product samples, boxed, 1930s. **$40-$45;** Calumet tin **$18-$20;** Baker's Coconut can **$15-$18;** Baker's Chocolate box **$10-$15**

Ekco/Ovenex Layer Cake Pan, aluminum, with label, 1950s, Ekco Products Co., Chicago, IL. **$12-$15**

Ekco/Ecolay Layer Cake Pan, with label, 1950s, Ekco Products Co. **$12-$15**

Mirro Spring-Form Pan, aluminum, "Clampless, for Tortes, Cakes, Desserts," boxed, 1950s, Mirro Aluminum, Manitowoc, WI. **$20-$25**

Mirro Layer Cake Pan, aluminum, "Loose bottom for easily removing cakes," with label, 1950s, Mirro Aluminum. **$12-$15**

Mirro Cake Pan, aluminum, "Bakes all 3 perfectly, Chiffon, Sponge Cake, and Angel Food," with label, 1950s, Mirro Aluminum. **$18-$20**

Bake King Layer Cake Pan, with label, 1960s, Alcan Metallic, Lake Zurich, IL. **$8-$12**

Tier Cake Pan Set, "So easy to make a beautiful 4-tier cake," boxed, 1950s. **$20-$25**

Saturday Evening Post, May 21, 1955, with cover illustration by Stevan Dohanos. A discouraged lass is shown in her modern kitchen losing the battle with an uncooperative cake.

Rudolph the Red Nosed Reindeer Cake and Mold Pan Set, 8 pieces, copyright 1939, Robert L. May, boxed, 1950s, Bake King, Chicago Metallic Mfg. Co., Chicago, IL. **$45-$55**

Lamb and Bunny Set, 10-piece
aluminum, boxed, 1950s, Blue Ribbon
Bakeware, Downers Grove, IL. **$25-$30**

Checkered Marble Cake Pan Set, boxed, 1940s, Chicago Metallic Mfg. Co., Chicago, IL. **$22-$25**

Heart Cake and Mold Pan, with label, 1950s, Bake King, Chicago Metallic Mfg. Co. **$18-$20**

Tree Cake Pan, tin plate, with label, 1950s,
Bake King, Chicago Metallic Mfg. Co. **$18-$20**

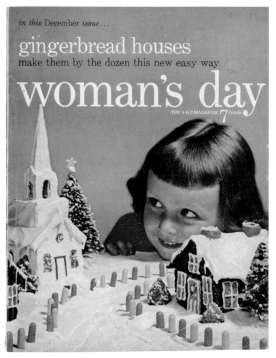

Woman's Day, December 1955, issue features gingerbread houses made from aluminum house molds. **$6-$8**

Alumode Gingerbread House Mold, mentions *Woman's Day* article on box, with cardboard sleeve, 1950s, Aluminum Specialty Co. **$22-$25**

Holiday Gingerbread House Cake Form, four-piece snap-apart, in package, 1950s, Mirro Aluminum, Manitowoc, WI. **$22-$25**

Mirro All-Purpose Molds, set of eight, "For shortcakes, salads, etc.," boxed, 1950s, Mirro Aluminum. **$18-$20**

Easy-Out Ring Mold, "for perfect molds everytime!," boxed, 1940s, West Bend Aluminum Co., West Bend, WI. **$18-$20**

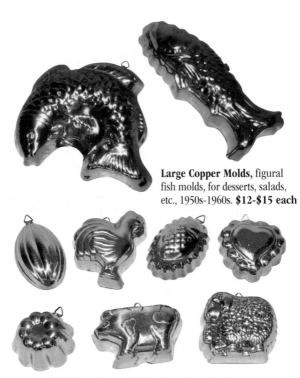

Large Copper Molds, figural fish molds, for desserts, salads, etc., 1950s-1960s. **$12-$15 each**

Miniature Copper Molds, figural molds, for desserts, salads, etc., 1950s-1960s. **$6-$8 each**

Mirro Mold Set, small, six pieces, copper-toned aluminum set, "For salads, gelatins, etc.," boxed, 1950s, Mirro Aluminum. **$25-$28**

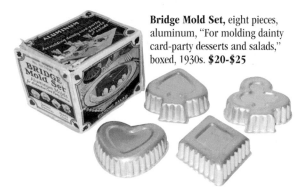

Bridge Mold Set, eight pieces, aluminum, "For molding dainty card-party desserts and salads," boxed, 1930s. **$20-$25**

Chapter 5

Cake Covers, Cake Decorations and Accessories

Cakes are a special treat associated with happy events such as weddings, birthdays, and many other celebrations. Through the years, manufacturers have catered to the needs of cooks who want to give their cakes a special design or treatment by producing a wide assortment of items. Vintage accessories for decorating, trimming, cutting, and carrying cakes are increasing in popularity with collectors. In many cases, these products and their packaging illustrate the enthusiasm for the event being celebrated, making them fun to collect.

Saturday Evening Post, January 3, 1953, with cover illustration by Norman Rockwell. The portly chef is reading up on his diet while munching on a low-calorie meal, but one wonders how long he can keep it up surrounded by all those luscious cakes. **$15-$20**

Cake Cover,
metal, yellow lid
with apple design.
Same pattern was
used on canister
sets, flour sifters,
etc., 1940s-1950s.
$22-$25

Cake Cover,
aluminum lid with
wood acorn handle
and embossed side
pattern, 1950s, West
Bend Aluminum
Co., West Bend,
WI. **$18-$22**

Cake Cover, metal with Pennsylvania Dutch design lid, small size shown, 1940s-1950s. **$18-$22;** large size **$22-$25**

Cake Cover, green-toned aluminum, "Musicake," rotating base music box plays Happy Birthday, boxed, 1950s, Heller Hostess-ware, White Plains, NY. **$35-$40**

Cake Cover, locking copper-tone aluminum with painted base, wooden handle, and cake graphic, 1950s, Mirro Aluminum, Manitowoc, WI. **$22-$25**

Cake Cover, locking styrene plastic with graphic design, 1950s-1960s, Federal Plastic Housewares, Chicago, IL. **$18-$22**

Cake Cover, copper-tone aluminum with plastic handle and cake graphic, 1950s, West Bend Aluminum Co. **$15-$20**

Cake Cover, locking copper-tone aluminum, square with wooden handle, boxed, has tag, 1950s Mirro Aluminum. **$30-$35**

Cake Cover, styrene plastic with clear "locklift" lid and embossed design, 1950s, Trans Spec Co., Cleveland, OH. **$22-$25**

Cake Cover, styrene plastic with yellow "locklift" lid and embossed design, 1950s, Trans Spec Co. **$18-$22**

Better Homes and Gardens, March 1952, small boy, who is probably more interested in sampling than mixing, tastes a frosting that is lickin' good! **$6-$8**

Cake Server, Kut-n-Serve, metal with plastic handles, "No fumbling, no crumbling," boxed, 1950s, Krag Steel Products, Chicago, IL. **$15-$18**

Hostess Cake Caddy, metal with brown, marbled Bakelite handles, boxed, 1950s, Lagner Mfg. Co. **$15-$18**

The American Magazine, May 1937, cover photo by Paul Hesse, shows two kids blowing out the candles of a birthday cake. **$6-$8**

Cake Servers,
orange plastic with
fluted handle, 1950s,
Rogers Plastic Corp.,
W. Warren, MA.
$2-$5

Green plastic with
molded design,
1950s, marked
Tico. **$10-$12**

Red plastic with knob
controlled gripper,
hand-painted
design, marked
St. Petersburg, FL,
1950s. **$15-$18**

**Celebration Toast
Glasses,** set of 12,
"For every occasion,"
boxed, 1950s, Maude
B. May Co., Chicago,
IL. **$12-$15**

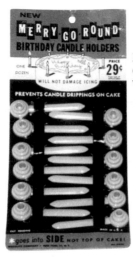

Merry-Go-Round Birthday Candle Holders, in package, Wecolite Co., New York, NY. **$6-$8**

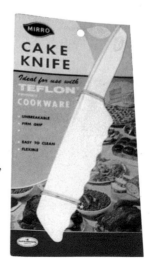

Mirro Cake Knife, unbreakable, flexible plastic, on card, 1960s, Mirro Aluminum, Manitowoc, WI. **$12-$15**

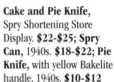

Cake and Pie Knife, Spry Shortening Store Display. **$22-$25; Spry Can,** 1940s. **$18-$22; Pie Knife,** with yellow Bakelite handle, 1940s. **$10-$12**

Shape A Cake, Santa form for cutting cake shape, boxed, 1950s, Fox Run Craftsmen, Ivyland, PA. **$18-$20**

Aluminum Cake Decorator, with four tips, "Add the caterer's touch," boxed, 1940s-1950s. **$12-$15**

Pierre Plastic Chef with metal rod, on card, 1950s, Hamblin Mfg. Co., Worcester, MA. **$12-$15**

Saturday Evening Post, June 16, 1945, with cover illustration by Stevan Dohanos. This cake is obviously for a returning serviceman's wedding, and the calendar in the background showing bread being lifted gives the sense that prosperity awaits the happy couple. **$8-$10**

Mirro Decorating Set, aluminum with six tips, "For cakes, cookies, pastries, etc.," boxed, 1950s, Mirro Aluminum. **$15-$18**

Aluminum Cake Decorator, Happy Birthday, "for delightful, interesting cakes," with six tips, boxed 1940s, Made in USA. **$18-$20**

Chapter 6

Can Openers

Collectors may want to ask what came first, the can or the can opener? It's not hard to reason that a can came first, however, the first can opener, a simple puncturing and cutting device was not far behind. Vintage can openers from the 1930s to 1960s offer collectors a large assortment, varying in design and complexity. Standard types were either handheld or wall mounted, with manufacturers adding extra features, such as magnetic lid catchers to deluxe models. Prices for the most part remain reasonable, and many collectors search for examples that complement their other kitchen collectibles.

Saturday Evening Post, February 28, 1953, with cover illustration by Constantin Alajalov. A critical moment during home economics class, the instructor taste testing has everyone's full attention. However, the prognosis for the sauce is poor. **$8-$10**

Canmaster Can Opener, chromed
metal with bracket, 1950s. **$8-$10**

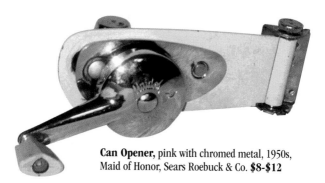

Can Opener, pink with chromed metal, 1950s,
Maid of Honor, Sears Roebuck & Co. **$8-$12**

Can Opener, turquoise with gold-toned metal, 1950s, Swing-A-Way, St. Louis, MO. **$8-$12**

Fint Wall Can Opener, chromed metal with magnet lid lifter, boxed, 1950s, Ekco Products Co., Chicago, IL. **$18-$22**

Edlund "Top-Off" Jar Opener, metal with wood handle, "Loosens the toughest jar caps," 1940s-1950s, Edlund Co., Burlington, VT. **$8-$10**

Edlund Jr. Can Opener, metal with wood handle, self puncturing, 1940s-1950s, Edlund Co. **$12-$15**

Flint Wall Can Opener, chromed metal with bracket, opens square or round cans, boxed, 1950s, Ekco Products Co. **$12-$15**

Edlund "Flat-to-wall" Can Opener, metal with wood handle and built-in magnet, "Easy to use," boxed, 1950s, Edlund Co. **$22-$25**

Flex Roll Wall Can Opener,
with magnet attachment,
plastic housing with metal,
in package, 1950s-1960s,
Vaughan Mfg. Co. **$22-$25**

**Safety Roll Jr. Can
Opener,** metal, "Opens cans
of all sizes, new modern
design," on card, 1950s,
Vaughan Mfg. Co. **$8-$10**

Vaughan's Smoothcut Can Opener,
plywood store display, holes in board originally
held demonstration unit. **$45-$65**

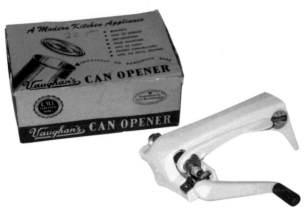

Vaughan's Smoothcut Can Opener, metal, "A modern kitchen appliance, beautiful, easy to operate," boxed, 1940s-1950s, Vaughan Mfg. Co., Chicago, IL. **$35-$40**

J&L Steel ad featuring can openers from the *Saturday Evening Post,* April 30, 1955. This housewife opening cans blindfolded is so giddy about it, you're sure the men in the white coats can't be too far off! **$2-$5**

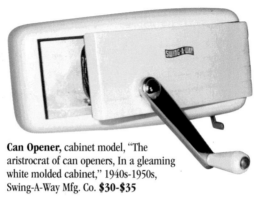

Can Opener, cabinet model, "The aristrocrat of can openers, In a gleaming white molded cabinet," 1940s-1950s, Swing-A-Way Mfg. Co. **$30-$35**

Wall-Type Can Opener, chromed-metal with plastic knob, with carton, 1940s-1950s, Swing-A-Way Mfg. Co. **$30-$35**

Can and Bottle Opener, metal with plastic knob, geared, "Swings flat against the wall," boxed, 1940s, Steel Products Mfg. Co. **$15-$18**

Wall Can Opener, metal and plastic, with magnetic lid lifter, boxed, 1960s, Swing-A-Way Mfg. Co. **$15-$18**

Kwik-Kut Jr. Can Opener, chromed metal with plastic handle, "Always handy, Always ready," boxed, 1950s, Dazey Corp. **$18-$20**

Deluxe Can Opener, red metal with chrome, 1950s, Dazey Corp. **$18-$22**

Canaramic Can Opener, turquoise metal and chrome, with magnetic lid lift, "Complements the modern kitchen décor," boxed, 1950s, Dazey Corp., St. Louis, MO. **$25-$30**

Super Senior Can Opener, white metal with chrome, boxed, 1950s, Dazey Corp. **$22-$25**

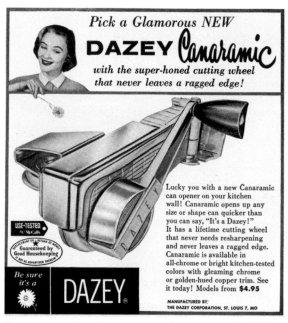

Dazey Canaramic ad from *Good Housekeeping*, November 1957.

12

* Whether You're Mixing a Batch of Batter....Opening Cans
* Crushing Ice Cubes....Or Sharpening Knives and Scissors
* Dazey Does an Expert, Efficient Job for You

A Egg Beater. Blends, whips or beats! Stainless steel high speed blades designed for easier cleaning. Quiet, smooth-running action; adjustable handle for right or left hand use. Chrome finish with enameled handle and knob in red, yellow or black. **12A $5.95**

Be sure *it's a* DAZEY

DAZEY KITCHEN HELPS ...
PRACTICAL TO GIVE AND TO OWN

B Table-Topper Dual Electronic Can Opener. Designed for portable use. Large rubber vacuum cup allows mounting on table, work counter and other areas of non-porous material such as formica, glass, porcelain or stainless steel. Exclusive height adjustment. Lid lifter holds cut-off can lids. In red, white or yellow. Specify color. **12B $7.95**
Table-Topper Can Opener. Like (B) but minus Lid Lifter. **12B1 $6.95**

C Triple Ice Crusher. Instantly adjusts to crush ice fine, medium or coarse for use in beverages, sea food, ice bags. Stainless steel cutters; white baked enamel body. Durable transparent plastic ice cup and handle knob in red, yellow or black. **12C $9.85**
Triple Ice Crusher with all-chrome body. **12C1 $10.95**

D Sharpit. Puts a sharp cutting edge on knives, scissors, other household tools. Dual wheels; guide for achieving perfect scissors bevel. Fits Dazey wall bracket. Red, yellow or white. **12D $4.25**
Sharpit. Same as (D), in Dazite non-rust finish. **12D1 $3.25**

E Dual Electronic Can Opener. Cuts out entire rims of round, oval and square cans; runs down rims. Swivel-mounted magnetic lid lifter holds cut-off can lids. Opener fits Dazey wall bracket, swings against wall when not in use. Red, white or yellow enamel finish with shining chrome trim. **12E $5.49** Without Magnet, **12E1 $4.49**
Dual Electronic Can Opener in Dazite non-rusting finish.
With Magnet, **12E2 $4.49** Without Magnet, **12E3 $3.49**

F Hold-Tite Magnetic Can Opener. Lighter version of Dual Electronic Can Opener. Magnetic lid lifter to hold cut-off lids. Fits Dazey wall bracket, swings back. Dazite non-rusting finish. **12F $3.25**
Hold-Tite Can Opener without magnetic lid lifter. **12F1 $2.85**

Catalog page from Warburg's Variety Store of Grand Rapids, Michigan, showing selection of Dazey products available in the 1950s. Catalog value: **$15-$18**

Can-O-Mat ad from *Saturday Evening Post,* June 11, 1960.

Can-O-Mat Can Opener, yellow metal with chromed handle, deluxe model with magnet and removable cutting blade, boxed, 1950s, Rival Mfg. Co., Kansas City, MO. **$28-$35**

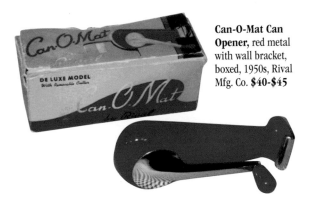

Can-O-Mat Can Opener, red metal with wall bracket, boxed, 1950s, Rival Mfg. Co. **$40-$45**

Can-O-Mat Can Opener, all chrome award model with 24K gold-plated handle, still sealed in its can, 1950s, Rival Mfg. Co. Curious packaging put a can opener in a can, thankfully it can be opened without using a can opener. **$75-$95**

Can-O-Mat Can Opener, turquoise metal with swinging bracket, 1950s. **$18-$22**

Rival Wall Can Opener, metal and plastic, "Its magnetic, It swings," in package, 1960s, Rival Mfg. Co. **$18-$20**

Can-O-Matic Electric Can Opener, pink
metal with chrome, 1950s-1960s. **$35-$50**

Swing-A-Way Can Opener, portable, chrome with plastic-coated handles, boxed, 1950s-1960s, Swing-A-Way Mfg. Co. **$12-$15**

Edlund Can Opener ad from *Good Housekeeping,* November 1951.

Edlund Can Opener ad
from *Good Housekeeping*,
November 1951.

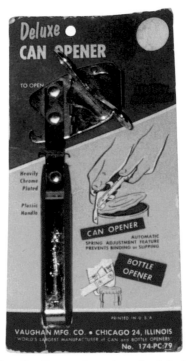

Deluxe Can Opener, chromed-metal and plastic, on card, 1950s, Vaughan Mfg. Co. **$15-$18**

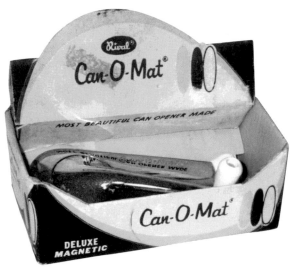

Can-O-Mat Can Opener, chrome metal with swinging bracket, boxed, 1950s-1960s, Rival Mfg. Co. **$22-$28**

Chapter 7

Canister Sets

Plastic canister sets, usually consisting of separate flour, sugar, coffee, and tea containers first became popular in the late 1940s. The advantages of bright colors, easily cleaned rounded corners, and low cost quickly made them preferable over wood, metal, or glass versions. Canister sets helped establish plastics in the kitchens of America and led to the acceptance of other products. Collectors usually look for sets that match their other collectibles or fit a chosen color scheme. Condition is important with mint examples considerably more desirable than those showing wear.

Lustro-Ware Sales Pamphlet, "Brightens kitchens, Lightens work," 1950s. **$30-$35**

Canister Set, four-piece styrene plastic, rectangular in turquoise with white lids and embossed metallic labels, 1950s-1960s, Beacon Plastics. **$18-$22**

Canister Set, four-piece styrene plastic, rounded corner design in pink and gray with integral handle lids and block lettering, 1950s, Burrite, Burroughs Mfg. Co., Los Angeles, CA. **$28-$35**

Popular Mechanics, October 1953, with cover illustration by Korta. Cover shows a 1950s couple in perfect harmony, he heads to the shop (in shirt and tie) and she goes to the kitchen. **$6-$8**

Plastic Canister/ Container, styrene plastic in pink and gray with lid, 1950s, Gitsware, Gits Molding Corp., Chicago, IL. **$12-$15**

Cookie Canister, red styrene plastic with white lid and lettering, 1950s. **$18-$22**

Salt & Pepper with Sugar Container, three-piece
styrene plastic set with hand-painted flower decoration,
1950s, Plastic Novelties Inc., Los Angeles, CA. **$22-$25**

Canister Set, three-piece styrene plastic, "The smart set for smart kitchens. The first and only canister set with a window, a feature to gladden any woman's heart," boxed, 1950s, Janetware Plastic Products, Aurora, IL. **$40-$45**

Popeil Canister Set, three-piece styrene plastic with red lids, 16 oz., 32 oz., and 64 oz., with labels, 1950s, Popeil Bros., Chicago, IL. **$30-$35**

Popeil Canister Set, three pieces, styrene plastic with clear lids and leaf design, 1950s, Popeil Bros. **$22-$25**

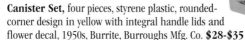

Canister Set, four pieces, styrene plastic, rounded-corner design in yellow with integral handle lids and flower decal, 1950s, Burrite, Burroughs Mfg. Co. **$28-$35**

Ice Bucket, styrene plastic with handle, lid and flower decoration, 1950s, Trans Spec Corp., Cleveland, OH. **$18-$22**

Canister Set, four pieces, styrene plastic, rounded-corner design in pink with gray knobs and kitchen decorations, 1950s-1960s, Burrite, Burroughs Mfg. Co., Los Angeles, CA. **$28-$35**

Canister/Cookie Jar, styrene plastic, rounded design with lid, 1950s, Burrite, The Burroughs Mfg. Co. **$22-$25**

Bread Box, styrene plastic, 1950s, Burrite, Burroughs Mfg. Co. **$15-$18**

Chapter 8

Crank-type Grinders, Salad Makers, Refrigerator Defrosters

Crank-type grinders and salad makers helped speed up production when preparing large quantities of food. Heat defrosters were used to combat the mass of ice that would frequently build-up around the freezer compartment of early refrigerators. Boxed versions with interesting graphics or colored aluminum add collector interest.

Magic Hostess Salad Chef and Meat Grinder page from a 1959
National-Porges merchandise catalog. Catalog value: **$18-$22**

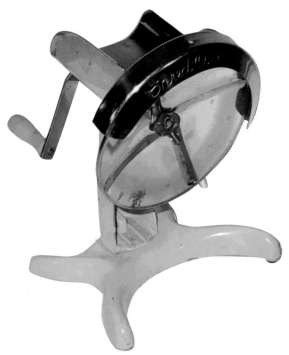

Shred-O-Mat Food Slicer, yellow metal with chrome top, attachments, and wooden handle, 1950s, Rival Mfg. Co. **$28-$35**

Saladeer Salad Maker, chromed metal, deluxe three cone with patented cone-grip lock, boxed, 1950s, Rival Mfg. Co., Kansas City, MO. **$20-$25**

Grind-O-Mat Meat Grinder and Food Chopper, chromed metal with attachments, boxed 1960s, Rival Mfg. Co. **$20-$25**

Grind-O-Mat, coral metal base with chrome top and wooden handle, 1950s, Rival Mfg. Co. **$35-$45**

Kitcheneer, white metal with chrome top, the Kitcheneer set included a Grind-O-Mat, shown, and a Shred-O-Mat with one mounting stand, 1950s, Rival Mfg. Co. **$35-$40**

Climax Food and Meat Chopper, metal, with
self sharpening cutters, boxed, 1950s, Universal,
Landers Frary & Clark, New Britain, CT. **$18-$22**

Magic Hostess Meat Grinder and Salad Chef,
chromed metal with attachments, boxed, 1950s,
Magic Hostess Corp., Kansas City, MO. **$22-$25**

Coffee-Mill, red metal and chrome top with clear plastic container and
wooden handle, wall mounted, "There's nothing like freshly ground coffee
for full-bodied flavor in every cup," boxed, 1950s, Rival Mfg. Co. **$50-$65**

WONDER-WORKING COOKING AIDS SAVE YOU TIME

FREE FOR FAMOUS TOP VALUE STAMPS

Page 60   *Special Order items—see page 97*

Page from a Top Value Stamps catalog showing a Shred-O-Mat,
Grinder, and other 1950s kitchen gadgets. Many of these items were
made of durable metals, and with care can continue to be used by
collectors without severely affecting their value. Catalog value: **$15-$18**

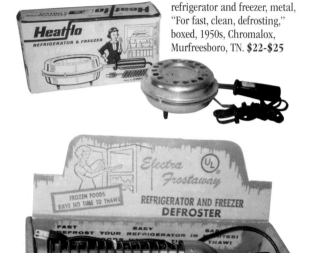

Heatflo Defroster, electric, for refrigerator and freezer, metal, "For fast, clean, defrosting," boxed, 1950s, Chromalox, Murfreesboro, TN. **$22-$25**

Electra Frostaway, for refrigerator and freezer, copper-toned metal with wooden handle, "Fast, Easy, Safe, Frozen foods have no time to thaw," boxed, 1950s. **$28-$35**

Ostrow 700 Defroster, infrared, metal with plastic handle, thermostat controlled, "Defrosting's a breeze," boxed, 1950s. **$20-$25**

Defrost King, plastic and metal defrost timer, "Set it, Forget it," boxed, 1950s, Galter Products Co. **$18-$22**

Bel-Air Super Defroster, 500 watt infra-red, color-toned aluminum with wooden handle, "Defrosts refrigerators and freezers without muss or fuss," boxed, 1950s, Bel-Air Appliances, Lynwood, CA. **$22-$25**

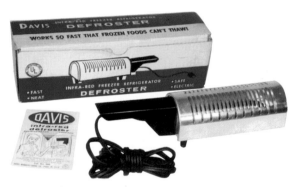

Davis Defroster, infra-red, for refrigerator and freezer, metal with plastic handle, "Works so fast that frozen foods can't thaw," boxed, 1950s, Davis Mfg. Co., Plano, IL. **$22-$25**

Chapter 9

Cookie Cutters

Collectors find the fun designs and shapes of cookie cutters hard to resist. The earliest cutters were fashioned from small scraps of tin or metal by hand. Manufacturers soon began producing designs to satisfy the needs and wants of users. Through the years, cookie cutters have evolved from all metal forms to stamped aluminum and molded plastic. The variety of shapes available is extensive with sets having illustrative packaging or boxes attracting the most collector interest.

Souvenir Program for the 10th annual Olympia
Circus, at the Chicago Stadium, 1942. **$18-$25**

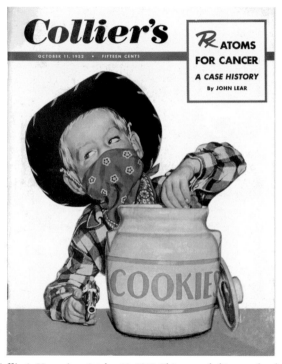

Collier's Magazine, October 11, 1953. This young lad in a cowboy hat makes a humorous image as he tries to hold up a cookie jar. **$8-$10**

Wonder Cutters, 12 assorted metal shapes, "For delightful sandwiches and cookies," boxed, 1930s-1940s, Kreamer Inc., Brooklyn, NY. **$18-$22**

Cake and Sandwich Cutters, metal bridge set "for luncheons and card parties," boxed 1930s-1940s. **$15-$20**

Barnyard Cookie Cutters,
12 metal animal figures,
boxed, 1950s. **$18-$22**

Cookie Cutters, 12 metal cutters "for all seasons,"
boxed, 1930s-1940s, GMT Co., New York, NY. **$18-$22**

Old Fashioned Cookie Cutters, 12 metal designs, "For cookies, canapés, etc.," boxed, 1950s. **$18-$22**

Miniature Cookie Cutters, six metal designs, boxed, 1950s. **$12-$15**

Miniature Cookie Cutters, six metal
Christmas designs, boxed, 1950s. **$12-$15**

Patriotic Cookie Cutters, four metal designs, "For celebrations and parties," boxed, 1950s. **$25-$30**

Trick or Treat Cookie Cutters, six metal Halloween designs, boxed, Ateco, August Thomson Co., New York, NY. **$40-$45**

Easter Cookie Cutters, six metal designs, "Also for cheese, thin breads, etc.," boxed, 1950s, Ateco, August Thomson Co., New York, NY. **$18-$22**

"Tala" Cookie Cutters,
12 metal shapes, boxed,
1950s, Taylor Law &
Co. Ltd., Stourbridge,
England. **$18-$20**

Cookie Cutter, 2 in 1, Snow Man or Gingerbread Boy, metal 8 in. high, "For all party occasions," boxed, 1950s. **$18-$20**

Cookie Cutter, Santa Claus, metal 8 in. high, "For all Christmas occasions," boxed, 1950s. **$18-$22**

Mirro Cookie Cutters, "In popular designs," in package, 1950s-1960s, Mirro Aluminum, Manitowoc, WI. **$12-$15**

Mirro Gingerbread Man, color-tone aluminum, on card, 1950s, Mirro Aluminum. **$18-$22**

Mirro Fairy Tale Cookie Cutter Set, five pieces, color-tone
aluminum, on blister card, 1950s, Mirro Aluminum. **$18-$20**

Holiday Cookie Cutters, five aluminum shapes, on card, 1950s, Color Craft, Indianapolis, IN. **$18-$22**

Mirro Cookie Cutters, six aluminum shapes, "In popular designs," in package, 1950s, Mirro Aluminum. **$18-$20**

Hansel and Gretel Cookie Cutter Set, five pieces, styrene plastic, boxed, 1947, Educational Products Co., New York, NY. **$35-$45**

Plastic Cookie Cutters, eight-piece set with figural animal shapes, boxed, 1940s, Hutzler Mfg. Co., Long Island City, NY. **$35-$40**

Christmas Cookie Cutter Set, nine pieces, plastic in holiday shapes, boxed, 1950s, Educational Products Co. **$22-$25**

3-D Cookie Cutter Set, eight plastic cutters make four animal-shaped cookies, 'That really stand up," boxed, 1950s, Wecolite Co., New York, NY. **$18-$22**

Circus Cookie Cutter Set, nine pieces, plastic, boxed, 1950s, Educational Products Co. **$35-$40**

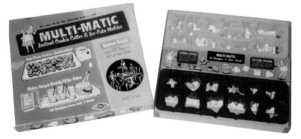

Multi-Matic Cookie Cutter and Ice Cube Maker, "Cuts clever cookies instantly," deluxe set with two cutters, boxed, 1950s. **$25-$28**

"Frigee-Maid" Ice Box Cookie Molds,
"easy to store, slice, and bake," boxed, 1950s,
Flambeau Plastics Corp., Baraboo, WI. **$22-$25**

Baking Sheet with Holiday Cookies Label, 1950s,
Bake King, Chicago Metallic Mfg. Co., Chicago. **$18-$22**

Chapter 10

Corn Gadgets

The popularity of corn, its unique shape, and its many eating and preparation methods have led to a host of products to make preparing and serving it easier. These include numerous servers, holders, butter applicators, and corn-shaped pans for baking. Other products have addressed the need to cut corn off its cob or to cream it. Collectors seek unusual and interesting items, or those that fit in with other kitchen collectibles. Corn's fun image has also resulted in many products having corn-themed graphics, creating great go-alongs for corn lovers.

Life Magazine, July 5, 1937. *Life Magazine*'s first year of publication included this feature about July corn on the cover. **$8-$10**

Griswold Corn Cake Pan, early American quality cast
iron, "There's nothing like iron to cook in," with cardboard
sleeve, 1950s, Griswold Mfg. Co., Sidney, OH. **$45-$50**

Corn Dishes, set of six aluminum, reusable with skewers, "Corn butters itself, Stays hot longer," in package, 1950s, E-Z-Por Corp., Chicago, IL. **$18-$20**

Chef's Corn Cribs, set of six aluminum with paper backing, "For cook-ins, For cook-outs," in package, 1963, Fluted Paper Products Co., S. Norwalk, CT. **$10-$12**

Kristy Korn Kob Pan, cast iron, "Makes delicious, Krunchy, krispy corn bread in a corn cob shape," with cardboard sleeve, 1950s, Wagner Ware. **$25-$30**

Serv-Rite Skewers and Corn Servers, plastic with metal pins, "Authentic cornhusk dishes," in package, 1950s. **$18-$20**

Lee Mfg. Co., Dallas, TX. The American Corn
Cutter, plastic with metal blade. boxed, 1950s-1960s,
American Corn Cutter Co., Cleveland, OH. **$10-$12**

Serv-Rite Corn Skewers,
with "no drip butter guard,"
in package, 1950s. **$10-$12**

"Beauty Bake" Corn Dish ad from
House Furnishing Review, May 1951.

"Beauty Bake" Corn Stick Dish, "Highest quality oven glass for baking or serving," with cardboard sleeve, 1950s, Miracle Maise Mills, Warsaw, IN. **$25-$28**

Hot Corn Holders, plastic, "Sterilize in washing like fine china," on card, 1950s, Sanford's, Bellwood, IL. **$10-$12**

Corn Butterer, set of four, stainless steel, boxed, 1960s,
Made in Japan, Viking Importrade, Moonachie, NJ. **$10-$12**

Corn Butter Brush, with nylon bristles, "No need to melt butter," on card, 1950s, W.F. Mayer Co., Yonkers, NY. **$12-$15**

Butter Brush, plastic, "Spreads butter easily," on card, 1950s, The Harwood Co., Farmingdale, NJ. **$12-$15**

Harwood's Corn Holders, plastic with stainless steel pins, on card, 1950s, The Harwood Co. **$12-$15**

Serv-Rite Corn Service Set, plastic, deluxe 18-piece set, "The modern way to serve corn on the cob," boxed, 1950s, Serv-Rite Corn Servers, Los Angeles, CA. **$25-$30;** Smaller sets without butter dish. **$18-$22**

Chapter 11

Donut Makers

Donut makers are a simple apparatus for dispensing batter, which became a popular kitchen accessory in the 1950s. The principle involves a spring-activated central plunger, which was held above a fryer to dispense batter in a uniform ring shape. Pancake batter can also be dispensed by the same method, and some of these devices were marketed as pancake makers. Most donut makers were made of aluminum or plastic and have a similar design and operating method. Many companies produced versions, and the plastic ones were offered in varying colors. Examples with their original box are of most interest to collectors. Many packages were saved for their recipes.

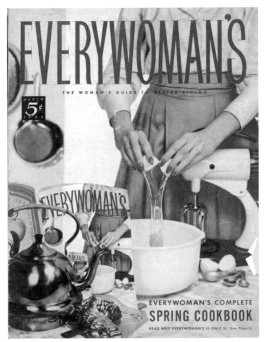

Everywoman's, March 1955, with an "infinity" kitchen image on the cover. Everywoman's was available at supermarkets in the 1950s for 5 cents a copy. **$6-$8**

New lightness! Full flavor! Truly digestible!

*What a **difference** when you change from ordinary frying fats to Crisco!*

Mmmm! What sweet treats doughnuts *can* be . . . so delicately crusted, so fluffy-light! But dollars to doughnuts you don't get that kind if you're frying with ordinary fat that has odor and flavor of its own. Such fat tends to *drown out* delicate flavor . . . may even give food a greasy flavor.

But oh, what a delicious difference when you change to all-vegetable Crisco for frying! It's so pure, so fresh. Crisco lets the delicate good flavor of foods come through while it browns them to perfection. See for yourself how different Crisco is. How white and creamy it looks! How sweet and fresh it smells! And how fresh it *keeps* without refrigeration!

Yes, Crisco lets you enjoy lighter, full-flavored fried foods. And 9 out of 10 *doctors* say Crisco-fried foods are easy to digest. Why, Crisco *itself* is digestible. So for flavor's sake, for *goodness'* sake, start now to fry with Crisco!

fry with
the one and only
Crisco
it's digestible

THE PROCTER & GAMBLE CO., makers of Oleo and Joy.

Crisco Shortening ad with donut recipe
from *Good Housekeeping,* April 1952. **$2-$5**

Essex Donut Maker, aluminum, "Makes two dozen donuts automatically," boxed, 1950s, Leyse Aluminum Co., Kewaunee, WI. **$18-$20**

Popeil's Donut Maker, plastic with wooden knob,
"Eliminates rolling, cutting, & forming donuts by hand,"
boxed, 1950s, Popeil Bros, Chicago, IL. **$18-$22**

Donut Cutter,
two pieces,
plastic, marked
Donut–Cooky Cutter,
1950s. **$5-$7**

Maid of Honor Donut Maker, aluminum, "Taste tempting donuts in a jiffy," boxed, 1950s, Sears Roebuck & Co. **$18-$20**

Mirro Donut Cutter, "Also for biscuits and cookies," on blister card, 1970s. **$6-$8**

Minit Chef, Pancaker, plastic with wood knob, "Holds 18, 4" pancakes," boxed, 1962. **$15-$18**

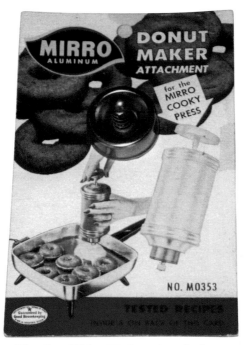

Mirro Donut Maker Attachment, anodized
aluminum, "For use with the Mirro cooky press,"
on card, 1950s-1960s, Mirro Aluminum. **$10-$12**

Mirro Donut Maker,
anodized gold
aluminum, "Easy to
use, makes 24 delicious
homemade donuts,"
boxed, 1960s, Mirro
Aluminum, Manitowoc,
WI. **$15-$18**

**Fairgrove Automatic
Donut Maker,**
aluminum, boxed, 1971,
Made in Hong Kong for
Aluminum Housewares
Co., Maryland Hts.,
MO. **$8-$12**

Alumode Donut Maker, aluminum, "The original donut maker," boxed, 1950s, Aluminum Specialty Co., Manitowoc, WI. **$18-$20**

Donut Master, aluminum, "Unbreakable, heatproof, fully automatic," boxed, 1950s, DRM Corp., Manitowoc, WI. **$18-$20**

"Tala" Doughnut Maker, aluminum with plastic handle
ring, "Delicious and so easy to make," boxed, 1950s,
Taylor Law & Co. Ltd., Stourbridge, England. **$20-$22**

Chapter 12

Egg Gadgets

Eggs are another area of food with its own specialized products and gadgets made to assist in preparation and serving. Whether you wanted to shell it, cook it, separate it, slice it, or even form it into a square, a product was made to aid you. Related items include egg cartons, eggcups, egg timers, etc. Collectors may want to have a few items that appeal to them or concentrate on one area. Eggs and their huge popularity have spawned a mini-industry of their own, and vintage egg-related items continue to increase in popularity.

"The Egg and I" sheet music, 1948,
Copyright Universal Pictures Corp. $8-$12

Egg Separator, plastic, "Place it over a cup and break the egg," on card, 1950s, The Harwood Co., Farmingdale, NJ. **$10-$12**

Egg Cooking Rack, aluminum, boxed, 1950s, West Bend Aluminum Co., West Bend, WI. **$12-$15**

Collier's Magazine, April 18, 1936, with cover illustration by Lawson Wood. The rooster seen here seems to be wondering why his nest hatchling is a "duck." **$8-$10**

"Tala" Egg Wedger, metal with wire cutting element, "Slices hard boiled eggs in the nicest way," boxed, 1950s, Taylor Law & Co. Ltd., Stourbridge, England. **$15-$18**

"Crax-Ezy" Boiled Egg Opener, plastic, "Stop making like Humpty Dumpty, No more burned fingers," in package, 1950s, M.P. Inc., Los Angeles, CA. **$10-$12**

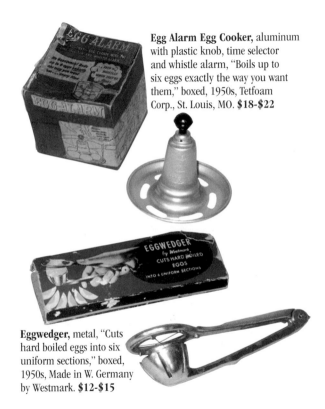

Egg Alarm Egg Cooker, aluminum with plastic knob, time selector and whistle alarm, "Boils up to six eggs exactly the way you want them," boxed, 1950s, Tetfoam Corp., St. Louis, MO. **$18-$22**

Eggwedger, metal, "Cuts hard boiled eggs into six uniform sections," boxed, 1950s, Made in W. Germany by Westmark. **$12-$15**

Egg Boiling Rack, aluminum, "Eggs boiled in upright position always have yolks in center," boxed, 1950s, Mullen Crafts Co., Evansville, IN. **$12-$15**

Small-Fry, set of two metal egg cooking frames, "For eggs at their best, Bastes, Fries, Poaches," boxed, 1949, The Benmatt Org., Chicago, Los Angeles. **$12-$15**

Egg Cuber, plastic, "Makes a square egg," boxed, 1977, Made in Hong Kong for Aluminum Housewares Co., Maryland Hts., MO. **$8-$10**

Eggcups, two-part plastic with hand-painted design, 1950s. **$12-$15 pair**

Egg Timer, plastic, "3 minute," "An absolute kitchen need," in package, 1950s, Del Ray Plastics Corp., New York, NY. **$30-$35**

"Jiffy Way" Egg Scale, metal with painted scale markings, 1940s, Jiffy Way Inc., Owatonna, MN. **$55-$65**

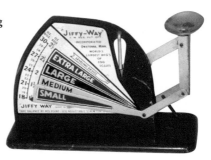

Slice Quickly, aluminum, "For vegetables, fruits, eggs," boxed, 1930s. **$15-$18**

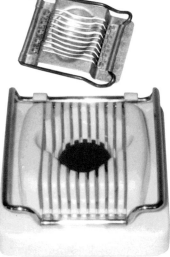

Egg Slicer, plastic and metal with red center, 1950s. **$8-$10**

Egg Cartons,
Farm Fresh from
Old Hickory
Smokehouse and
One Dozen Eggs,
Grade A Medium,
1950s-1960s.
$5-$8 each

Deluxe Egg Slicer,
plastic and metal,
"slices eggs in either
direction," on blister card,
1960s, Gemco Products,
Hewlett, NY. **$12-$15**

Egg Slicer, plastic and metal with round shape, 1950s-1960s, Medco, New York, NY. **$6-$8**

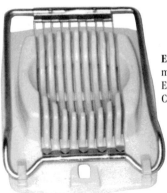

Egg Slicer, plastic and metal, 1960s-1970s, Ekco Products Co., Chicago, IL. **$6-$8**

Egg Slicer, Exquisit, aluminum,
boxed Wilesco (Germany) **$10-$12**

Prestige Sky-line Tomato Slicer, metal with wood handle, "For
tomatoes, cucumbers, eggs, etc.," with cardboard sleeve, 1950s. **$15-$18**

Plasmetl Egg Tray, styrene plastic, 1950s. **$12-$15**

Chapter 13

Flour Sifters

Flour sifters are a handy kitchen accessory for aerating flour and promoting even, lump-free baking. Sifters having a single screen with a simple rotating mechanism were developed in the 1920s, and later improvements, such as multiple screens and trigger-spring action, allowed better sifting and one-hand operation. Colorful printed metal designs from the 1940s and 1950s added appeal when new, and are still popular with collectors today. With flour sifters, the variety of designs produced over the years practically assures a match to anyone's kitchen decor or interest level.

Androck Flour Sifter, three screens, "Hand-I-Sift," red and white "Pantry Pattern" design with bakery items, 1950s. **$25-$30**

Androck Flour Sifter, three screens, yellow with
flower design and wood handle, 1940s. **$22-$25**

Now-with covers!

ANDROCK 3-SCREEN

Flour Sifter

Easier to fill . . . cleaner to store...stops leakage

Androck Sifter No. 773 has *everything*—3 screens . . . one-hand operation . . . new metal slip-on covers top and *bottom*. Easier to fill. No leaking. Shelf stays clean. Wonderful gift. Try its easy action at department, chain, hardware stores, super markets. $1.98.

ANDROCK

THE WASHBURN COMPANY, Worcester, Mass., Rockford, Ill.

ANDROCK
timesaving
FLOUR SIFTER

SIFT FLOUR JUST ONCE THROUGH 3 SCREENS

One hand does it! Get fluffier, lighter flour! 4-cup size.

Pantry Patterns	$1.89
Chrome sifter	$2.79

ANDROCK

QUALITY PRODUCTS SINCE 1880
THE WASHBURN COMPANY
Worcester, Massachusetts   Rockford, Illinois

Androck three-screen flour sifter ad from *Good Housekeeping*, June 1954.

Androck "Pantry Patterns" Flour Sifter ad from *Good Housekeeping*, November 1955.

Androck Flour Sifter, three screens, "Hand-I-Sift,"
wheat stalk and bakery items design, 1950s. **$25-$30**

Androck Flour Sifter, three screens with
geometric pattern, 1950s-1960s. **$15-$18**

"Sift-Chine" Flour Sifter, "guaranteed satisfactory,"
chrome with yellow bands, 1940s. **$18-$20**

Androck Flour Sifter, three screens, floral design
with wooden handle and knob, 1940s. **$22-$25**

Androck Flour Sifter, three screens, "Hand-I-Sift,"
mom and kids in the kitchen design, 1950s. **$35-$65**

Androck Flour Sifter, three screen with yellow
and red abstract design, 1960s. **$15-$18**

Androck Flour Sifter, three screen
in chrome, with label, 1950s. **$18-$20**

Flour Sifter, crank-type mechanism, strawberry design with wooden handle, unmarked, 1950s. **$18-$20**

Foley Flour Sifter, three screen in copper, marked Foley "Sift-Chine," with label, 1950s. **$25-$30**

"Sift-Chine" Flour Sifter, three screens with
wooden handle and knob, cream with orange bands,
1930s-1940s, Meets-A-Need Co., Seattle, WA. **$18-$20**

Androck Flour Sifter, one screen, three cup,
floral pattern, with label, 1950s. **$15-$18**

Flour Sifter, crank-type mechanism, daisy design
with wooden handle, unmarked, 1950s. **$18-$20**

Foley Flour Sifter, screen, with label, 1960s-1970s. **$8-$10**

Triple Screen Flour Sifter, three screen capacity, with label, 1960s, Aluminum Housewares Co., St. Louis, MO. **$15-$18**

Foley Flour Sifter, five cup, aluminum, comes apart to wash, with label, 1950s. **$28-$35**

Flour Sifter, triple screen, copper-toned, aluminum
and pink handle, with label, 1950s-1960s
Aluminum Housewares Co., St. Louis, MO. **$28-$35**

Flour Sifter, three screen, with label,
1960s, Bromwell Products. **$8-$10**

Flour Sifter, crank-type mechanism, apple
design with wooden handle, 1950s. **$20-$25**

Flour Sifter,
two cup,
styrene plastic
with metal
screen and
mechanism,
tea rose design,
1950s, no label
$15-$18; with
label **$18-$22**

Flour Sifter, five cup, styrene plastic with metal
screen and mechanism, flower design, and
graduations, 1950s, Popeil Bros., Chicago, IL. **$18-$22**

Chapter 14

Graters, Shredders, Slicers

Graters and shredders perform similar functions. Graters are better suited for cheese, chocolates, and harder foods, while shredders are usually reserved for lettuce or cabbage. Slicers are often used for tomatoes, potatoes, cheese, and similar foods. Most graters and shredders have a pattern of sharp-edged holes for producing fine, medium, or coarse food depending on the size of the hole. Slicers usually have a thin, sharp metal slot or wire to perform the cutting action. Devices range in complexity from simple handheld units to rotating tabletop models with interchangeable blade elements. A wide variety of graters, shredders, and slicers were produced over the years, with many companies offering special features or designs to have a competitive edge. Original boxes usually provided helpful instructions and recipes, and many were saved through the years. They typically feature interesting graphics and are sought after by collectors.

Saturday Evening Post, November 10, 1956, with cover illustration by Constantin Alajalov. A seat of gabbing girlfriends is shown eating to their hearts' content, while the matronly lady walking by doesn't seem to be very interested in the dietary fare on her own tray. **$8-$10**

"In-Genia" Folding Grater, with attached tray, "the greatest little grater you ever used," boxed, 1950s, Made in Italy, Overseas Housewares Co., New York, NY. **$15-$18**

Standfast Grating and Shredding Utensil, plastic with metal grating inserts, "the only shredder that doesn't fight back," boxed, 1950s, Standfast Products Co., Cleveland, OH. **$22-$28**

Acme Safety Grater,
"For easy dicing, grating,
straining," with insert sheet,
1950s, Acme Metal Goods
Co., Newark, NJ. **$12-$15**

Grater and Pan Set, "Grate right into the pan," boxed, 1950s, Elpo Industries Inc., New York, NY. **$15-$18**

Vitex Safety Grater, styrene plastic, "grate with safety," boxed, 1940s-1950s, a Renwal Product. **$15-$18**

Plasti-Grate, safe, sanitary, stainless, with attached card, 1950s, Nu-dell Mfg. Co., Chicago, IL. **$12-$15**

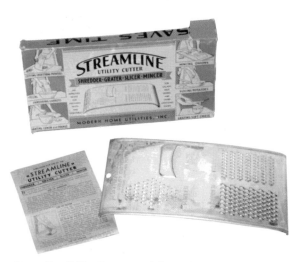

Streamline Utility Cutter, metal, "saves time, saves energy,'"
boxed, 1930s-1940s, Modern Home Utilities, Chicago, IL. **$22-$28**

Nu-Age Shredder Slicer, Grater, stainless steel, "Fully adjustable," boxed, 1950s, New-Age Products Co., Brooklyn, MI. **$18-$22**

Bromwell's Greater Grater, "Easy to use, For all grating purposes." with paper label, 1930s, Bromwell Wire Goods Mfg. Co., Cincinnati, OH. **$12-$15**

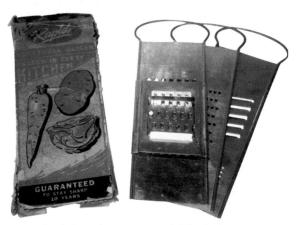

Rapid Salad Set, three pieces, metal, "Shreds, slices, grates," boxed, 1930s, Bluffton Slaw Cutter Co., Bluffton, OH. **$18-$22**

Rotary Food Grater, metal with wood handle, "It grates so many things in a jiffy" boxed, 1950s, Lorraine Novelty Mfg. Co., New York, NY. **$15-$18**

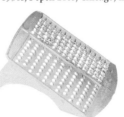

Safety Grate 'n Shred, styrene plastic, "Safe, compact, easy to clean," boxed, 1950s, Popeil Bros, Chicago, IL. **$18-$22**

Knapp's Safety Veg-e-grater, metal, boxed, 1930s, Knapp Monarch Co., Belleville, IL. **$18-$22**

Artbeck Dial-a-matic Shredder, "Easy, safe, at the turn of a dial," boxed, 1950s, Arthur Beck Co., Chicago, IL. **$18-$22**

Rapid Salad Set, metal, "Shreds, slices, grates, no slip, slide, or muss," boxed, 1950s, Bluffton Slaw Cutter Co., Bluffton, OH. **$18-$20**

Deluxe Dial-O-Matic Food Cutter, plastic with metal blade, "Slices, shreds, waffles, performs miracles with food," boxed, 1958, Popeil Bros., Chicago, IL. **$18-$22**

Tupperware Grater and Bowl, 1970s. **$10-$12.**

Slicer and Grater, plastic, 1950s-1960s,
Linda Foursome, made in USA. **$6-$8**

Slice-a-Way Shredder & Slicer, plastic unit with "3-way adjustable metal blade," boxed, 1950s, Popeil Bros., Chicago, IL. **$12-$15**

Mouli Salad Maker, metal with rotating grater elements, "Slices, chops, shreds," boxed, 1950s, Mouli Mfg. Co., Jersey City, NJ. **$18-$20**

Feemster's Famous Vegetable Slicer, metal with adjustable platform, boxed 1940s-1950s, W.R. Feemster Co., Brooklyn, MI. **$15-$18**

The New Rotary Mouli Grater, with "Removable drum for easy cleaning," boxed, 1950s, Mouli Mfg. Co., Jersey City, NJ. **$12-$15**

Speedy All Purpose Slicer, "Faster, easier, amazing new kitchen aid," boxed, 1950s, Tower Hall, Chicago, IL. **$12-$15**

Chapter 15

Kitchen Clocks

A wide selection of fun kitchen clocks were made from the 1940s to 1960s. The major companies, Telechron-General Electric, Sessions, Westclox and others, strove to outdo one another by continually introducing new, visually appealing models. Most were made primarily of plastic, however, other materials such as ceramics and metals were also used. Collectors find that a vintage clock makes an interesting accent piece with figural shapes or special designs appealing to many. The relatively few collectors concentrating solely on clocks allows ample opportunity to satisfy individual preferences. With kitchen clocks, style, color, and condition are important factors affecting value. Versions used in a display need not work, but top dollar is usually reserved for working examples.

General Electric Clock ad from
Woman's Day, December 1951. **$2-$5**

Telechron "Telechoice" Shelf or Wall Clock, styrene plastic with metallic waterfall ends, 1950s. **$35-$40**

Telechron Kitchen Clock, styrene plastic with metallic wrap-around center sections, 1940s-1950s. **$45-$50**

Telechron Clocks ad from *Saturday Evening Post,* 1950s, Telechron div. of the General Electric Co., Ashland, MA. **$2-$5**

Telechron Kitchen Clock, styrene plastic
with rounded front corners, 1950s. **$22-$25**

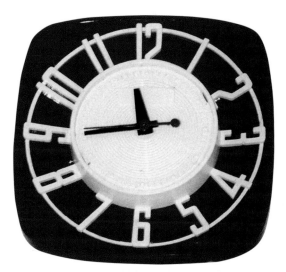

Telechron Clock, styrene plastic with smaller
rounded-off square design, 1950s. **$22-$25**

Telechron Clock, styrene plastic with
rectangle shape, 1950s-1960s. **$22-$25**

Telechron Clock, styrene plastic, "floating"
bubble clock design with an outer numeral band,
1950s, in yellow with black numerals. **$45-$50**

Telechron Clock, styrene plastic, "floating" bubble clock design with an outer numeral band, 1950s, in red with white numerals. **$65-$75**

General Electric Clock, styrene plastic, with
perimeter scallop design, 1950s-1960s. **$22-$25**

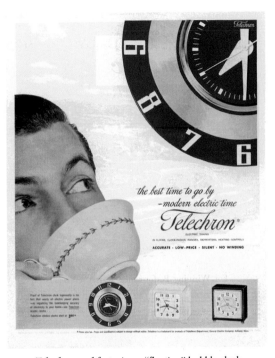

Telechron ad featuring a "floating" bubble clock design, from *Better Homes and Gardens*, October 1953, Telechron div. of General Electric Co.

Spartus Clock, styrene plastic, with numeral "pods" protruding from center section, 1950s, Herold Products Co., Chicago, IL. **$40-$45**

Westclox "Manor" Clock, styrene plastic in rectangular design, 1950s-1960s, Westclox, LaSalle, IL. **$22-$25**

General Electric Clock, pink and white
styrene with clear cover, 1950s. **$25-$28**

Westclox "Wallmate" Clock, smaller styrene plastic square design with round clock center, 1950s, Westclox, LaSalle, IL. **$22-$25**

Sunbeam Clock, styrene plastic, round design
with squared numeral backgrounds, 1960s,
Sunbeam Products Co., Chicago, IL. **$12-$15**

General Electric "Clansman" Clock, styrene plastic with plaid background design, "Lends new glamour to any kitchen's color scheme," 1950s. **$22-$25**

Sessions Kitchen Clock, plastic teapot-shaped design, 1950s, Sessions Clock Co., Forrestville, CT. **$55-$60**

Sunbeam "Kitchenette" Clock, styrene plastic, "Add beauty to your kitchen," in package, 1950s-1960s, Sunbeam Products Co. **$25-$28**

Sessions Kitchen Clock, plastic "Pierre" chef-shaped design, 1950s, Sessions Clock Co. **$50-$55**

Seth Thomas Apple Clock, styrene plastic with
painted leaves and stem, 1950s, Seth Thomas Clocks,
div. of General Time Corp., Thomaston, CT. **$45-$55**

United Pocket Watch Clock, plated brass
housing with metal chain, 1950s. **$65-$75**

Kit Cat Klock, styrene plastic, battery operated with moving eyes and tail, 1950s, California Clock Co., San Juan Capistrano, CA. **$35-$50**

Ceramic Kitchen Clock, designed by Russel Wright with General Electric movement, 1950s. **$65-$75**

Chapter 16

Lustro-Ware/Columbus Plastic Products

In Columbus, Ohio, a struggling plastics molding firm was taken over by an eager Harvard graduate, Gebhard W. Keny. This change was the nucleus for the start of Columbus Plastic Products. Early product designations, such as the Zippo line, fell by the wayside in favor of the Lustro-Ware name. The introduction of a molded styrene plastic cutlery tray in the 1940s revolutionized its entire product category. The future of Columbus Plastics Products seemed bright. After the creation of an in-house design department, other innovative products were introduced. One of the first was a plastic canister set having a simple straightforward design, block lettering, and rounded, easy-to-clean inside corners. This set was followed by a line of matching pieces including bread boxes, shakers, and dispensers that helped set a uniform modern style for American households. The basic colors of red and yellow were augmented by other hues, so that the products from Columbus Plastics fit right in with the ongoing color schemes of the day.

Columbus Plastic Products and Lustro-Ware continued to be a leader in the 1950s and diversified into polyethylene items and larger molded pieces such as laundry baskets, trash containers, and other household necessities. Their main facility on Mound Street in Columbus, Ohio, more than tripled in size within a span of a few years. By the late 1950s, most of the products were being made in the softer shades of pink, turquoise, and light yellow. Continued success with plastics molding innovation resulted in the development of intricate molds capable of making lacey napkin holders and plastic doilies available at five and dime stores for 19 cents. In its heyday, the Lustro-Ware line boasted the availability of "Over 100 stylized items to brighten the home."

The classic design period at Columbus Plastic Products ended around 1959, when the more abstract lettering and designs of the Elegante line were introduced. In a sense, the simplicity of the product shape seemed to be upstaged by the ornate graphics, and the overall effect didn't seem to work as well. However, the Lustro-Ware line continued to be successful and still featured older as well as new products. In 1966, Columbus Plastic Products was acquired by the Borden Company. After additional product changes, including the adoption of avocado green and harvest gold to its color palette, Lustro-Ware's design direction while under Borden became diluted and did not recapture its former success.

Today, collectors seem drawn to the Lustro-Ware name, distinctly molded on the bottom of most of the products. The usual collecting pattern is for someone to acquire a canister set or other item and when a matching accessory piece is found, a collection is born. The most popular period for Lustro-Ware items spans roughly 1950 to 1960 and nearly any item from that time period in nice condition has collector interest. Most appealing are canister sets and other ensemble pieces with the classic block lettering bright and intact, and without cracks or other flaws. Expect to pay a premium price for boxed, mint-condition items and harder-to-find accessories like towel dispensers. Its not unusual for a Lustro-Ware "spice" rack, that is often used to display 1950s Aunt Jemima spice containers, to sell for upwards of $100 on the Internet and for period catalogs to do much better. But these items are the exception, and with the number of objects in circulation, Lustro-Ware is truly a collectible available for anyone showing an interest.

Lustro-Ware Colander, boil-proof rigid polyethylene, "Will not mar sink," with label, 1950s. **$20-$25**

Zippo Utility Line, plastic encased "For kitchen, bathroom, basement, etc.," boxed, 1940s, Columbus Plastic Products Co. **$22-$25**

Lustro-Ware Clothesline, stock #R1, "Convenient, practical, for drying hosiery, lingerie, etc.," boxed, 1950s. **$22-$25**

Lustro-Ware Egg Trays, compact, 12 egg capacity, 1950s. **$18-$22**

Lustro-Ware Spice Cabinet, "Holds eight to ten cans of spices," with insert card, 1950s. **$35-$40**

Lustro-Ware Relish and Bread Tray, styrene plastic, with label, 1950s. **$18-$22**

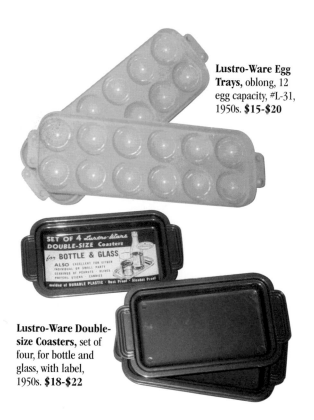

Lustro-Ware Egg Trays, oblong, 12 egg capacity, #L-31, 1950s. **$15-$20**

Lustro-Ware Double-size Coasters, set of four, for bottle and glass, with label, 1950s. **$18-$22**

Lustro-Ware, America's Foremost Line, front cover from 1951 Lustro-Ware Catalog, collection of Internet seller Marsha Brandom. Catalog with letter, price list, and envelope. **$125-$150**

Lustro-Ware Ice Bucket, double wall styrene plastic with lid, #112, 1950s, in brown & cream **$18-$22;** red & white. **$22-$28**

Lustro-Ware Watering Can, styrene plastic
with clear bottoms, #P-10, 1950s. **$25-$30**

Lustro-Ware Bread Box, #B20L, 1950s. **$35-$45**

Lustro-Ware Recipe Box, styrene plastic, #B-25, 1950s. **$22-$25**

Lustro-Ware Canister Set, mint set, 1950s. **$40-$55**

Lustro-Ware Salad Tongs, styrene plastic, #T-40, "Exclusive one piece spring action design," with label, 1950s. **$18-$25**

Lustro-Ware Salt & Pepper Shakers, small table size, "Easy to fill twist-lock covers," #SS-2, mint set. **$12-$15**

An assortment of items shown in a 1950s *Lustro-Ware Catalog.* Customers sending for a free catalog also received a price list and available mail-order outlets.

Lustro-Ware Refrigerator Set, three-piece, "safe, guaranteed unbreakable for 1 year," Red with styron labels, if in package, **$25-$28**

Lustro-Ware Pie Box, clear styrene marked made in USA, #B-40, "keeps pie tasty fresh," with label, 1950s-1960s. **$18-$20**

Lustro-Ware Paper Towel Holder, styrene plastic, spring action brackets, #H-10, "durable, economical, convenient," on card, 1950s. **$15-$18**

Lustro-Ware Paper Towel Holder, later version 1950s-1960s. **$10-$12**

Lustro-Ware Loop Towel Holder, styrene plastic, #L-27. Saves space, decorative, for kitchen or bathroom, on card, 1950s. **$18-$22**

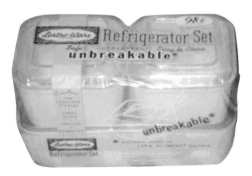

Lustro-Ware Refrigerator Set, three-piece, safe, guaranteed unbreakable for 1 year, in package, yellow, 1950s. **$25-$30**

Front cover from mid-1950s Lustro-Ware catalog. Catalog
with letter, price list, and envelope. **$125-$150**

**Lustro-Ware
Refrigerator Pitcher,**
two-piece styrene
plastic body with swing
action lid, 2 quart
capacity, #L-45, 1950s.

Green, unused with
early sticker **$25-$30**

Yellow, with sticker
$22-$28

Lustro-Ware Table Pitcher, styrene
plastic, #L-46, solid yellow, 1950s. **$18-$22**

Lustro-Ware Table Pitcher, styrene plastic, blue and white with transfer decoration, 1950s-1960s. **$15-$20**

Ad page showing National Hardware Association approved Lustro-Ware store display from *Hardware Age*, mid-1950s. **$20-$22**

Lustro-Ware, full-color ad showing products available in 1959, *Hardware Age*. **$15-$18**

Lustro-Ware full-color ad from 1959 shows the Elegante
Metallic Leaf design, *Hardware Age*. **$15-$18**

Chapter 17

Measuring Spoons and Cups, Timers, Scales, and Adders

Measurement aids are a practical kitchen accessory. Cooks need to know how much of an ingredient to use, or have a way to time a cooking process. Many varieties of measuring cups, spoons, timers, and scales have been produced over the years, and manufacturers were quick to adapt features that set their products apart. Measuring sets were bound together or a wall rack was provided to make them handier to use; special designs, such as adjustable models or double-sided wet and dry measures, were created.

Many companies added color or novel design shapes to increase interest. Collectors today will find a range of vintage measures, timers, and scales of interest, and can concentrate on examples that match their other kitchen collectibles.

Saturday Evening Post, February 19, 1955. This cover, by Amos Sewell, shows an eager group of kids making a raid on a well-stocked refrigerator. **$8-$10**

Kitchen Gift Set, deluxe set with measuring spoons and cups, S&P shakers, and mixer, boxed, 1950s, Color Craft, Indianapolis, IN. **$85-$95**

Wonder Cup, plastic measuring device, "For the particular housewife, takes the guesswork and messwork out of cooking," boxed, 1950s, Milmour Products, Chicago, IL. **$12-$15**

"Long 'n' Lovely" Measure Set, aluminum with plastic-coated handles, "they're simply beautiful and so handy," on card, 1950s, Magic Hostess Corp., Kansas City, MO. **$25-$30**

Measurettes, four "spun ray" aluminum measuring cups, boxed, 1950s. **$15-$18**

Tala Cooks Measure Funnel, aluminum with printed design, 1950s, Taylor Law & Co. Ltd., Stourbridge, England. **$18-$20**

Tallscoops Measuring Spoons, four colored aluminum spoons with rack, "a bright addition to any kitchen," boxed, 1954, Ray Walther Co., Des Moines, IA. **$35-$45**

Mirro Measuring Spoon Set, color-tone aluminum, on blister card, 1950s-1960s, Mirro Aluminum, Manitowoc, WI. **$15-$18**

Ekco/Mary Ann Cooking and Measuring Set,
four pieces, aluminum, boxed, 1940s-1950s,
Ekco Products Co., Chicago, IL. **$18-$22**

Revere Ware Measuring Cup, boxed, 1950s, Revere Copper
and Brass Inc., Rome Mfg. Div., Rome, NY. **$18-$22**

Woman's Day, July 1955. This laughing young lady has taken the idea of juggling kitchen activities to new heights. **$6-$8**

Rooster Measuring Spoon and Hot Pad Holder, styrene plastic, with spoons, 1950s. **$22-$25**

Teapot Hot Pad Holder, styrene plastic, 1950s. **$15-$18**

Measuring Cups, aluminum with plastic handles, 1960s. **$12-$15**

Scoop Set, four pieces, mirror-finish aluminum, boxed, 1950s, Made in W. Germany by Westmark. Overseas Housewares Co., New York, NY. **$18-$20**

Measuring Cups, four pieces, multicolor polyethylene plastic, 1950s-1960s, Hutzler Mfg. Co., Long Island City, NY. **$12-$15**

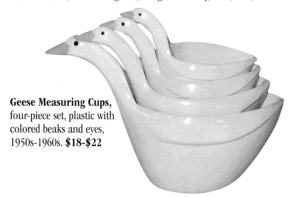

Geese Measuring Cups, four-piece set, plastic with colored beaks and eyes, 1950s-1960s. **$18-$22**

Measuring Spoons, four pieces, multicolor plastic, 1950s. **$8-$12 each**

Measuring Cup Set, four pieces, styrene plastic, "An indispensable utensil for canning," 1950s, Shel-Glo, Kilgore Mfg. Co. **$12-$15**

Lux Minute Minder, boxed, 1950s, Robert Shaw Controls Co., Waterbury, CT. **$18-$20**

Maid of Honor Household Timer, no winding necessary, boxed, 1950s, sold only by Sears Roebuck & Co. **$20-$22**

Mirro Matic Kitchen Timer,
"counts the minutes when
minutes count," boxed, 1950s,
Mirro Aluminum. **$22-$25**

Mirro Matic Timer, gold-
toned aluminum, 1950s,
Mirro Aluminum. **$15-$18**

American Family Scale, with food graphics and plastic weigh platform, 1960s-1970s. **$18-$20**

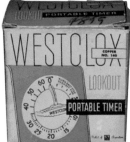

Westclox Portable Timer, copper and plastic, boxed, 1950s, Westclox, General Time Corp., LaSalle, IL. **$18-$22**

Small Home Builders Year Book, 1939. Cover illustration shows couple gazing into a crystal ball to view their home of the future. Magazine features a demonstration home from the 1939 New York World's Fair. **$8-$10**

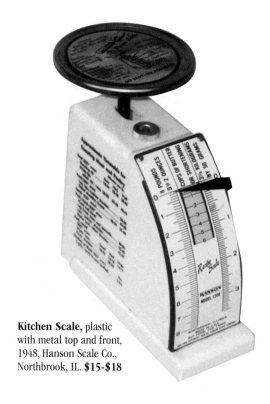

Kitchen Scale, plastic
with metal top and front,
1948, Hanson Scale Co.,
Northbrook, IL. **$15-$18**

American Family Scale,
metal with gray and white
dial, 1950s, American Family
Scale Co., Chicago. **$15-$18**

Kitchen Scale,
aluminum top bowl with
plastic bottom, marked
"House Proud," registered
design, 1950s. **$22-$28**

Super Add-A-Matic Supermarket Adder, 1950s. **$10-$12**

"Dan-Dee" Add-kwik Supermarket Adder, in package, 1950s. **$15-$18**

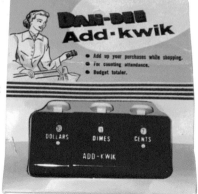

Chapter 18

Patty Shell Molds, Fry Pan Shields

Patty shell molds are used to deep fry batter into various shapes. A metal form is dipped in batter, deep fried, and the mold is removed to form a crispy batter shell. A typical set includes several differing shapes and a holding rod. A variety of sets were produced over the years as fried batter shells were a common party or luncheon treat. Many patty shell mold sets were kept in their original boxes for storage and to retain enclosed recipes. Collectors search for interesting examples and items having mint-condition boxes.

Saturday Evening Post, April 18, 1953, with cover illustration by John Falter. There isn't much these young cooks haven't experimented with when mom was outside, won't she be surprised! **$8-$10**

Griswold Patty Molds, cast iron, boxed,
1950s-60s, Griswold Mfg. Co. **$22-$25**

Griswold Famous Patty Molds, cast iron, "For tempting, delicious, desserts, salads, etc.," boxed, 1950s. **$28-$35**

Handi-Hostess Kits. Jumbo Deep Fry Molds or Waffle Plate, Hors D'Oeuvre Molds, cast aluminum with wood handle. boxed, 1950s, Bonley Products Co., Chicago, IL. **$15-$18**

8 in 1 Hostess Mold-er-ett, cast aluminum with wood handle, "For Appetizers, Desserts, Hors D'Oeuvres," boxed, 1950s, Bonley Products Co. **$15-$18**

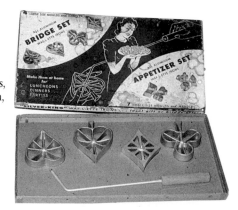

"Silver King" Bridge Set, Waf-l-ette Irons, cast aluminum, boxed, 1950s, Silver King Corp., Aurora, IL. **$15-$18**

"Silver King" Luncheon Set, Waf-l-ette and Patty Shell Moulds, cast aluminum, 1950s, Silver King Corp. **$15-$18**

Nordic-Ware Double Rosette & Timbale Iron,
cast aluminum, boxed, 1960s-1970s, Northland
Aluminum Products Inc., Mnpls, MN. **$10-$15**

Nordic-Ware Double Rosette & Timbale Iron, cast aluminum, "Two molds per dip," boxed, 1950s, Northland Aluminum Products Inc., Mnpls, MN. **$15-$18**

French Waffler, aluminum with plastic handles,
"French Waffles in a Jiffy, fits right in your toaster!"
boxed, 1950s, Fred Stuart Corp., New York, NY. **$18-$22**

Filter-Fry, aluminum with Bakelite knob, "Takes the spatter out of frying," boxed, 1940s-1950s. **$20-$22**

Fairgrove Spatter-Prufe, aluminum, "Keeps spatter in, lets steam out," in package, 1971, Made in Japan for Aluminum Housewares Co., Maryland Hts., MO. **$10-$12**

Magic Hostess Spatter-Prufe, aluminum, "Nothing like it anywhere, Lets all the steam out, keeps all the spatter in," in package, 1957, Magic Hostess Corp., Kansas City, MO. **$18-$20**

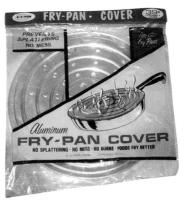

Fry-Pan Cover, aluminum, "No spattering, No mess, No burns," in package, 1950s-1960s, E-Z-Por Corp., Chicago, IL. **$18-$20**

Patty Shell Set, aluminum, on blister card, 1960s, Made in Japan for Harbor Co., Aurora, IL. **$8-$10**

Chapter 19

Pie Pans, Rolling Pins, Cookie and Pastry Presses, Accessories

Pie baking has many dedicated enthusiasts who enjoy the preparation as well as the taste of the final product. Mastering the various steps and techniques is an art, always subject to a special process or step an experienced cook might want to add. Over the years, manufacturers have created numerous pans, rolling pins, presses, crimpers, etc., to help improve results and make the process easier and more fun. Collectors search for unusual or decorative examples and find that a few vintage rolling pins or pastry accessories make great additions to any kitchenware collection.

Saturday Evening Post with cover illustration by Stevan Dohanos. A 1950s mutual swap rest break is shown, pie for milk and milk for pie. Seems like an idyllic exchange to me. **$8-$10**

Fire King 9" Pie Plate, "Bake serve store and reheat in the same dish," with label, 1950s, Anchor Hocking, Lancaster, OH. **$15-$20**

Pyrex Flavor Saver Pie Plate, "Keeps the juice and flavor in your pie!" with label, 1950s, Corning Glass Works, Corning, NY. **$15-$20**

Bake-King 9" Pie Plate, orange pie recipe, with label, 1950s, Chicago Metallic Mfg. Co., Lake Zurich, IL. **$12-$15**

Bake-a-Pie, Metal Rim Baking Plates, "Perfect for frozen pies," with label, 1950s, Sutherland Paper Co., Kalamazoo, MI. **$10-$12**

Bake-King Save All Pie Plate, "Saves the pie juices, Keeps the oven clean," with label, 1950s. **$12-$15**

Pyrex 10" Pie Plate, "bake, serve, freeze, all in one dish," with label, 1960s. **$10-$12**

Lattice Pie Cutter, styrene plastic, "Ok'd by experts, Used by housewives, The new modern way to make lattice pies," red on large card, 1950s, Kesco Plastics, Chicago, IL. **$15-$18**

Lattice Pie Cutter, styrene plastic, clear with paper label. **$10-$12**

"Take-a-Long" Covered Pie Pan, with label, 1950s, Aluminum Housewares Corp., St. Louis, MO. **$15-$18**

"Criss Cross" Lattice Pie-Top Cutter, styrene plastic, "makes perfect lattice–top pies!" in package, 1950s, Clough Products, Prairie Village, KS. **$18-$22**

KVP Pie Tape, "Keeps the juice in the pie," boxed, 1950s, Kalamazoo Vegetable Parchment Co., MI. **$10-$12**

Gold Medal Pie Crimper, metal, "Makes pies the easy way," boxed, 1950s. **$18-$22**

"Bake-an'-Take" Covered Cake Pan, with label, 1950s, Aluminum Specialty Co., Manitowoc, WI. **$15-$18**

Ceramic Pie Plates, Apple & Cherry, pie recipes printed under glazing, 1960s. **$12-$15 each**

Nayco Ripple Rolling Pin, "For cookies, pies, cakes, and breads," boxed, 1950s. **$25-$30**

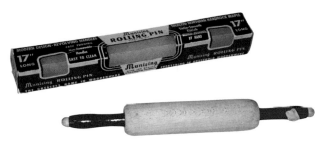

Munising 17" Rolling Pin, "modern design" with "selected northern hardrock maple," boxed 1940s-1950s. **$22-$25**

Lokstad Die-cut Rolling Pin, "For cookies, pastries, flatbreads," 1950s, Lokstad Products, Newfolden, MN. **$18-$25**

World's Fair Rolling Pin, "For smooth rolling with a feather touch," with wrapper, 1950s, Forster Mfg. Co., Farmington, ME. **$22-$25**

Krispy Krust Rolling Pin, chrome, with catalin plastic handles and ball bearings, 1940s, Buffalo Toy and Tool Works, Buffalo, NY. **$40-$45**

Everywoman's Magazine, September 1954. Covers with only food items, like the favorite fruit pies shown here, were a recurring theme in the 1950s. **$6-$8**

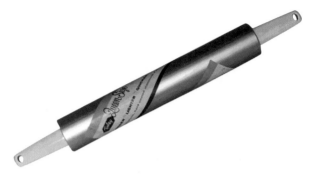

Queen Size Rolling Pin, aluminum with plastic handles, "Rolls more tender dough," with label, 1950s-1960s, Foley Mfg. Co., Mnpls, MN. **$22-$25**

Ekco Rolling Pin, pink with green and chrome accents. **$35-$45**

Ekco Rolling Pin, selected hardwood, with sleeve,
1950s, Ekco Products Co., Chicago, IL. **$15-$20**

Ekco Rolling Pin, plastic, yellow with
red and chrome accents, 1950s. **$30-$35**

Nevco Rolling Pin, hardwood with ball bearings, with label, 1950s, Nevco Products Inc., Yonkers, NY. **$22-$25**

Ekco Rolling Pin, hardwood, with label, 1970s. **$12-$15**

Ekco Rolling Pin, anodized aluminum, "High styled for brighter baking," boxed, 1950s. **$45-$55**

Foley Pastry Frame, with rolling pin cover, wood and canvas, with label, 1950s, Foley Mfg. Co., Mnpls, MN. **$22-$25**

Happy Home Rolling Pin, hardwood with nylon bearings, with label, 1960s, Woolworth's. **$15-$18**

Welmaid Pastry Cooks' Canvas, with rolling pin sleeve, boxed, 1950s. **$10-$12**

Ateco Magic Cookie Maker, Cake Decorator, "Makes cookies in a jiffy," boxed, 1930s-1940s, August Thomson Co., Brooklyn, NY. **$22-$25**

Pastry Cloth and Rolling Pin Cover, "Makes rolling of dough easier and faster than ever before," in package, 1950s, H&P House Furnishing Co., Fairlawn, NJ. **$12-$15**

Edith Hansen's Pastry Cloth, with rolling pin coverlet, "A household necessity, Makes baking a pleasure," in package, 1951, The Perflex Co., Shenandoah, IA. **$8-$10**

Cookie Sheet Liners, eight liners, "For perfect cookies every time!" in package, 1950s, Superior Insulating Tape Co., St. Louis, MO. **$8-$10**

Ateco Cookie and Noodle Maker,
"Stimulate your artistic inclinations," boxed,
1950s, August Thomson Co. **$18-$20**

Mirro Cooky & Pastry Press, 15 fancy shapes and wood rack, "Makes 80 cookies in one filling," boxed, 1950s, Mirro Aluminum, Manitowoc, WI. **$22-$25**

MIRRO
THE FINEST ALUMINUM

cooky-pastry press

mother likes MIRRO *best!*

COOKIES, CREAM PUFFS,

ECLAIRS, LADY FINGERS,

MERINGUES

SO *Easy* TO MAKE . . .

AND *Decorate*

...smart cookies.

And smart little sisters, too, to turn out such smart-looking cookies this easy, twist-of-the-wrist way.

The MIRRO Cooky and Pastry Press turns baking touch to magic . . . makes cooky-making a pleasure . . . gives professional results every time.

All sets packaged in colorful display boxes, with dustfree Mylar windows.

MIRRO COOKY-PASTRY PRESS

Just a turn of the handle creates fancy cookies, lady fingers, eclairs, cream puffs or meringue shells

Set consists of 12 interchangeable forming plates for making fancy cookies, plus 3 easy-to-use pastry tips. Stain-resisting AIumilite with lustrous Copper-Tone trim. Comfortable turning grip. Directions and recipes included.

Number	Gauge	Diam.	Height	Ship. Unit	Weight Ship. Unit
358AM	20	3″	7¾″	6 only	9 lbs.

Packed in individual 4-color display cartons, then repacked in corrugated shipping carton.

33

Mirro Cooky & Pastry Press as
shown in a 1950s catalog. **$18-$20**

Aluminum Cooky Press, with four forming plates, boxed, 1940s, Made in USA. **$18-$20**

Simplicity Cooky Press, four designs, "For thick or thin cookies," boxed, 1930s-1940s. **$15-$18**

Wear-Ever Cookie Press, 12 shapes, "Sensational no-guess measure knob," boxed, 1950s, Aluminum Cooking Utensil Co., New Kensington, PA. **$18-$22**

Mirro Cooky Press, "New easy grip, With 12 fancy shapes," boxed, 1940s-1950s, Mirro Aluminum. **$22-$25**

Mirro Cooky & Pastry Press, "For cookies, éclairs, cream puffs, etc.," boxed, 1950s, Mirro Aluminum. **$18-$22**

Cooky Press, styron plastic, six metal inserts with cake decorator attachments, boxed, 1950s, Popeil Bros., Chicago, IL. **$18-$20**

Cookie Press and Cake Decorator, "See-It" transparent plastic, boxed, 1950s, Wecolite Co., New York, NY. **$22-$28**

Gadget Master Cookie Press, styrene plastic, "Enjoy making cookies at home," boxed, 1950s, Popeil Bros., Chicago, IL. **$15-$18**

Mirro Cookie Kit, "Dial-a-Cookie," pastry press with three rotating disks, makes 12 designs, in package, 1960s, Mirro Aluminum. **$18-$22**

Cookie Chef and Pastry Gun, aluminum and plastic, six design tips, trigger operated, boxed, 1960s, West Bend Aluminum Co., West Bend, WI. **$15-$18**

Cookie Chef and Pastry Gun, aluminum, "Trig-a-matic," boxed, 1950s, Vital Products Mfg. Co., Cleveland, OH. **$15-$18**

Cookie King, crank-type, cookie press spritz gun, copper-toned aluminum, boxed, 1950s. **$20-$22**

Wear-Ever Cookie Gun and Pastry Decorator, with thickness control, boxed, 1960s, Made in Japan for Wear-Ever Aluminum, Chillicothe, OH. **$15-$18**

Nutbrown Cookie and Biscuit Maker, aluminum, boxed, 1950s, Thos. M. Nutbrown Ltd., Blackpool, England. **$12-$15**

**Wear-Ever "Lazy Suzy" Cookie Cutter
Wheel,** aluminum with styrene plastic
center, "Newest easiest way to make
fancy cookies every day," boxed, 1950s,
Aluminum Cooking Utensil Co. **$22-$25**

Ekco/Mary Ann Cookie and Sandwich Cutter, cuts six different
shapes, boxed, 1950s, Ekco Products Co., Chicago, IL. **$12-$15**

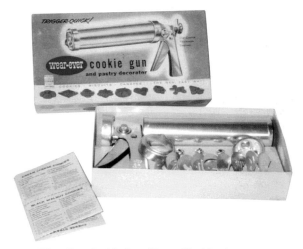

Wear-Ever Cookie Gun, "For cookies, biscuits, canapes, with cookie thickness dial, Trigger quick!" boxed, 1950s, Aluminum Cooking Utensil Co. **$18-$22**

Wear-Ever Cookie Gun and Pastry Decorator ad, *McCalls*, November 1957. $2-$5

Spry Shortening ad, with 5 on 1 Cookie Cutter Wheel promotion, from *Woman's Day*, November 1953. **$2–$5**

Spry Cookie Cutter Wheel Store Placard, 1950s. **$15-$20;** Spry Shortening Can, 1950s. **$15-$20;** Spry 1950s Cookie Wheel. **$15-$18**

Rotating Cookie and Sandwich Cutter, "Cuts five attractive shapes with one easy motion," boxed, 1950s, Overseas Housewares Co., New York, NY. **$15-$18**

Mechanical Cookie Cutter, metal, "Cuts dozens of cookies in seconds, No more one at a time!" boxed, 1940s-1950s, Syndicate Sales, Mnpls, MN. **$20-$22**

Cookie Cutter Wheel, aluminum with plastic handles, 1950s, Foley Mfg. Co., Mnpls, MN. **$8-$10**

Cookie Cutter Wheel, three-shape rotating plastic with wooden handle, 1950s. **$8-$10**

Saturday Evening Post, September 23, 1957, with cover illustration by Constantin Alajalov. Portly gentleman is shown with heaping plates of food in both hands and no place to sit. **$8-$10**

Chapter 20

Potato Cutters, Choppers, Corers, Etc.

Specialty cutters, choppers, and corers provide useful kitchen functions, including making french-fries, dicing onions and vegetables, coring apples and fruits, etc. Numerous examples were produced by manufacturers and innovative marketers through the years, and many of these same products continue to be made in modern versions today. Examples include rotating food choppers from the 1950s, and one-piece apple corers that could core and section an apple in one motion. Choppers and cutters appeal to kitchenware collectors who want a variety of objects having a specialized purpose.

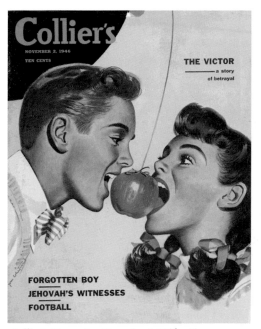

Collier's Magazine, November 2, 1946, with cover illustration by Jon Whitcomb. The young folks on the cover will probably have a hard time with this apple. They should try one of the apple gadgets shown in this section. **$8-$10**

Blitzhacker Lightning Food Chopper, plastic with metal cutting blade, "Does the job just by tapping, Original Swiss design," boxed, 1950s, New-Nel Kitchen Products, Chicago, IL. **$18-$22**

The New Villa French Fry Potato Cutter, metal with wood handle, "Strongest and safest," boxed, 1940s, Made in England. **$22-$25**

Maid of Honor French Fry Potato Cutter, metal with wood handle, "Fast, convenient," boxed, 1950s, sold only by Sears Roebuck & Co. **$18-$20**

Presto French Fry Cutter, metal, "Cuts a whole potato at one time, safe as a simple toy," with attached card, 1950s, M.E. Houck, Cincinnati, OH. **$10-$12**

Ekco French Fry Potato Cutter, metal with plastic handle, 1960s, Ekco Products Co., Chicago, IL. **$8-$12**

Nutbrown Chipper and French Fry Cutter, metal with wooden handles, simple to operate, "The finest of all chippers!" boxed, 1940s, Thos. M. Nutbrown Ltd., Blackpool, England. **$25-$28**

Huot Serrater and Meat Tenderizer, stainless steel with plastic handle, "Give your salads a new zip," with sleeve, 1950s, Huot Mfg. Co., St. Paul, MN. **$15-$18**

Federal Onion Choppers, regular, painted metal with wooden knob, graduated, with label, 1940s **$25-$28**

Mrs. Damar's Potato Cutter, metal with natural wood handle, "Cuts 25 french fries in one stroke," boxed, 1950s, Damar Products Co., Newark, NJ. **$20-$22**

Sky-line Miracle Chopper, "automatically rotating stainless steel blades," boxed, 1950s. **$20-$22**

"Chop-o-matic" Food Chopper, plastic with automatic rotating stainless steel blades, "Just tap it," boxed, 1956, Popeil Bros., Chicago, IL. **$18-$22**

The Avon Giant Size Rotomatic Food Chopper, plastic with stainless steel blades, boxed, 1950s, Avon Products Co. **$20-$22**

Roto Chop, giant automatic food chopper, "Steel blades rotate as they chop," boxed, 1958, Popeil Bros., Chicago, IL. **$18-$20**

Tearless Onion, Vegetable, and Nut Chopper, metal and wood top with glass cup, with label, 1940s-1950s, Acme Metal Goods Mfg. Co. **$18-$20**

Chopper, vegetable and nut meats, decorated metal and wood top with graduated glass container, 1950s. **$12-$15**

Automatic Food Chopper, metal and plastic top with graduated glass container, 1950s. **$12-$15**

Food Chopper, plastic with steel blades, 1950s. **$12-$15**

Tearless Onion and Vegetable Chopper, stainless steel blades, metal and wood knob with glass container, with label, 1940s-1950s, Acme Metal Goods Mfg. Co., Newark, NJ. **$15-$18**

Merry Go Round Food Chopper, plastic with wood top knob, 1950s. **$12-$15**

Food Chopper, stainless steel blades with wooden handle, 1940s. **$12-$15**

Chopper, Stainless Steel with Plastic Handle, "Meat tenderizer, chopper, dicer," with sleeve, 1950s, The Turner and Seymour Mfg. Co., Torrington, CT. **$18-$22**

"Chop' n Slice," chopper, stainless steel, "Slices, dices, chops," on blister card, 1964, made in Japan for Nevco, Yonkers, NY. **$8-$10**

Deluxe, perforated aluminum top with wooden knob, graduated, with label, 1940s. **$28-$35**

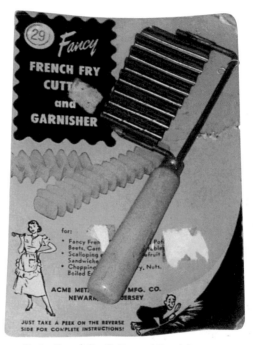

Fancy French Fry Cutter and Garnisher,
metal with wooden handle, on card, 1950s, Acme
Metal Goods Mfg. Co., Newark, NJ. **$12-$15**

Kwik-Kut "The ideal food chopper," stainless steel with tooth edge, boxed, 1950s, Kwik-Kut Mfg. Co., Mohawk, NY. **$10-$12**

Kitchen Chopper, stainless steel, "Comfortable, natural grip," with insert card, 1950s. **$10-$12**

Apple Slicer and Corer, metal, "Eight slices in one stroke," on card, 1976, Kitchen King, Central Islip, NY. **$6-$8**

Apple and Pear Corer, Slicer, metal, "Makes fruit serving a pleasure," on card, 1950s, Turner and Seymour Mfg. Co. **$12-$15**

Hostess Wire Slicer, metal slices thick or thin, the "All purpose slicer for cheese, butter, eggs, etc.," on card, 1960, A Kenberry Product, John Clark Brown Inc., Belleville, NJ. **$12-$15**

Cheese Slicer, stainless steel with easy grip wooden handle, "Ideal for ice cream, butter, bananas, eggs, etc.," on card, 1950s, The Turner and Seymour Mfg. Co., Torrington, CT. **$15-$18**

The Kwik Kut Cheese Slicer, metal and wood, "Slices butter, ice cream, eggs, etc.," on card, 1950s, Uebel Mfg. Co., Bellevue, KY. **$12-$15**

Cheese Slicer, rust proof metal and plastic, "For butter, eggs, and many others," on card, 1950s, Vaughan Mfg. Co., Chicago, IL. **$12-$15**

Citra Grapefruit Corer, serrated stainless
steel with wooden handle, on card, 1950s,
Citra Products, Winter Haven, FL. **$15-$18**

Real-a-Peel Parer and Corer, metal, "The household knife of many uses," on card, 1940s-1950s Tarrson Co., Chicago, IL. **$15-$18**

Vitex Corer, for fruits and vegetables, plastic with wooden handle, "Makes the fruit appear delightfully attractive & appetizing," boxed, 1950s. A Renwal Product, made in USA. **$10-$12**

Bean-X, "Stems, strings, slices, beans stay greener, taste better," boxed, 1950s, G.N. Coughlan Mfg. Co., West Orange, NJ. **$10-$15**

Rosebud Radish Cutter, styrene plastic, "Makes radish roses simply and easily—no skill needed," on card, 1950s, Nudell Plastics. **$12-$15**

Saw Knife, miracle stainless steel serrated edge, "For frozen food, poultry, etc.," boxed, 1950s, Saw Knife Co., Chicago, IL. **$8-$10**

Home Smorgasbord Knife, "Beautiful design with Swedish steel blade," boxed, 1950s, Simmons Slicing Knife Co., Chicago, IL. **$12-$15**

Amazing Peel King, electric peeler with stainless steel blades, pares, peels, slices, etc., "Wife saver, does the work for you!" boxed, 1950s-1960s, S&H Mfg. Co., Cleveland, OH. **$25-$35**

Gadget Master Grapefruit Knife, stainless
steel with plastic handle, "For preparing
grapefruit and orange segments," on card,
1950s, Popeil Bros., Chicago, IL. **$18-$20**

Duol Frozen Food Knife, stainless steel, "The
perfect kitchen robot, does everything, cuts,
saws, slices, serves!" boxed, 1950s. **$12-$15**

Blue Ribbon Carving Set, stainless steel with stag-pattern handle, boxed, 1950s. **$18-$22**

Famous Coronet Carving Set, stainless steel with plastic handles, boxed, 1950s, E.C.L., New York, NY. **$18-$20**

Veri-Sharp, stainless kitchen cutlery, with a Wondawood handle, on card, 1960 Imperial Knife Co., Providence, RI. **$8-$10**

Households Serrated Paring Knife, stainless steel with hardwood handle, on card, 1950s. **$8-$10**

Lightning Action Ice-Cream Scoop, stainless with plastic handle, "A necessity for the smart housewife." boxed, 1950s, Kam kap Inc., New York, NY. **$35-$45**

Scoop Master Ice-Cream Scoop, "For modern serving, for every kitchen," boxed, 1950s, Bonny Products Co., New York, NY. **$35-$45**

Bi-Cor Ice-Cream Scoop, stainless with plastic handle, "For ice cream, potatoes, sandwiches," boxed, 1950s, Bloomfield Industries, Chicago, IL. **$20-$25**

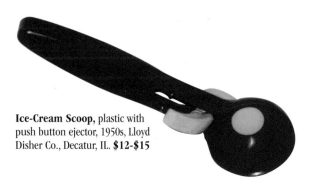

Ice-Cream Scoop, plastic with push button ejector, 1950s, Lloyd Disher Co., Decatur, IL. **$12-$15**

Quick Mayonnaise Maker, steel with glass housing, "Made expressly for the Wesson Oil people," boxed, 1940s-1950s, Wesson Oil, New Orleans, LA. **$25-$28**

Automatic Butter Curler, two-piece
metal unit, boxed, 1960s, made in
Japan for Chadwick Miller. **$10-$12**

Saucy Melter, melts butter, cheese, sauces, "No scorching, No burning, No watching," boxed, 1950s-1960s, Aluminum Housewares Corp., St Louis, MO. **$12-$15**

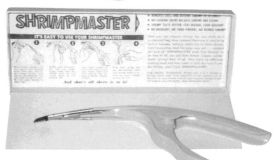

Shrimpmaster, plastic and metal, "No drudgery, no tired fingers, no ruined shrimp," boxed, 1950s. **$12-$15**

Chapter 21

Rubbermaid

In the late 1920s, two executives at the Wear-Ever division of the Aluminum Corporation of America, Horatio Ebert and Errett Grable, decided to purchase the Ohio-based Wooster Rubber Co. At the time, Wooster Rubber was making toy balloons, gloves, and other items from latex rubber, but was failing to show much of a profit. The new ownership team helped revive the operation, but by the Depression years of the early 1930s it was paramount that new products be developed for the company to thrive.

At about the same time, James Caldwell, a rubber chemist formerly with the Seamless Rubber Co., had created an innovative colored-rubber dustpan and several other products. Initially turned down by retail outlets, since a rubber dustpan would sell at $1 versus the standard 39 cents, Caldwell set about marketing his dustpans door to door with encouraging results. This effort led to the first Rubbermaid store sales and drew the attention of Ebert and Grable at the Wooster Rubber Co. James Caldwell's expertise with rubber products and sales acumen fit closely into their need for growth. Combining Caldwell's Rubbermaid operation into the Wooster Rubber Co. proved beneficial to both parties.

By the 1930s, sales of dustpans, sink strainers, a molded steel-wool pad holder, and other household products became the primary source of revenue at the Wooster Rubber Co. A new manufacturing facility was opened, and in the 1940s new products, stressing innovation and quality, such as a rubber-coated dish drainer led to increased sales. In the mid-1950s, items molded out of polyethylene, starting with a sink strainer, were added to the line. In 1957, Rubbermaid Inc. became the official company name. The 1960s, and later, saw the adoption of rotating lazy susans, food storage containers, and shelving systems, further expanding Rubbermaid sales and product categories.

Today, older Rubbermaid items appeal to many collectors of vintage kitchenware. For those who want to create a retro kitchen, a few Rubbermaid items from the 1950s help enhance the overall look, particularly when colors are matching. Recently, 1960s items in turquoise and other colors have shown strong buyer interest during Internet auctions.

Rubbermaid Shelf Kushions, "To beautify and protect your shelves permanently," boxed, 1950s. **$22-$25**

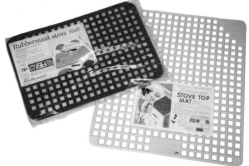

Rubbermaid Stove Top Mats, "Provides extra cushioned work space while preparing meals," in package, 1950s, small **$25-$28**; large **$25-$30**

Rubbermaid Steel Wool Holder, "Protects hands and nail polish," on card, 1950s. **$15-$18**

Rubbermaid Dustpan, 1950s. **$22-$25**

**Rubbermaid Sink
Divider Mat,** with
card insert. **$22-$25**

Rubbermaid Colorful Coasters,
set of eight, 1950s. **$15-$18**

Rubbermaid Lazy Susan Canister Set, turquoise, styrene plastic, 1960s. **$25-$30**

Rubbermaid Lazy Susan Canister Set, styrene plastic, 1970s. **$12-$18**

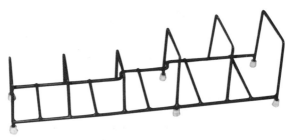

Rubbermaid Plate Rack, large size, "Keeps cupboards neat–
Conserves space and provides handy access," 1940s-1950s. **$18-$22**

**Rubbermaid
Utensil Trays,**
polyethylene,
blue with script
logo, 1950s.
$12-$15

Chapter 22

Salt and Pepper Shakers

The seemingly unlimited variety of plastic salt and pepper shakers made enable collectors to easily focus on subjects of interest or concentrate on certain types. Although the stature and cost of vintage shakers have increased substantially from their dime store origin, they can still be considered a sort of collectible bonbon, pleasant and enjoyable, but not particularly rare. For collectors, boxed versions and fanciful designs increase interest with the use of wall displays providing a typical way to showcase collections. For plastic salt and pepper shakers, the emphasis remains on the fun with other collecting benefits an added bonus.

Spicer-ette Dispenser, six compartments, styrene plastic, "Handy, compact, sprinkles or pours, Spice supply always visible," boxed, 1950s, Spicer-ette Co., San Francisco, CA. **$22-$25**

Magic-Spray Salt and Pepper Servers, styrene plastic with push button mechanism, boxed, 1950s, Magii Products Inc., Rockford, IL. **$18-$20**

Cat and Dog Salt and Pepper Shakers, styrene plastic with painted details, promotional set from Ken-L Ration dog food, 1950s, marked F&F Tool and Die, Dayton, OH. **$25-$28**

Salt and Pepper Shakers with Teapot Wall Hanger, styrene plastic, 1950s, Superlon, Chicago, IL., and W. Stephens Mfg. Co., Los Angeles, CA. **$22-$25 set**

Egg-shaped Salt and Pepper Shakers, styrene plastic with clear base, with mailing carton, 1950s. **$18-$22**

Penguin Pals Salt and Pepper Set, fluted glass body with plastic head and tuxedo, boxed, 1950s, D'Art Craftsman Corp., New York, NY. **$25-$28**

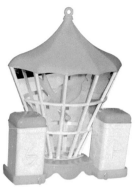

Salt and Pepper Shaker Set, styrene plastic with wall hung, gazebo-like cage design, 1950s, Superlon, Chicago, IL. Add **$8-$10** for earlier version with two color cage, bird and background mirror. **$18-$22**

Pear Salt and Pepper Set, styrene plastic with painted details and holder, 1950s, made in USA. **$20-$22**

Kitten Salt and Pepper Shakers, styrene plastic, painted details, 1950s, add **$5-$8** if plastic holder is included. **$15-$18**

Humpty Dumpty on Wall Salt and Pepper Shakers, styrene plastic with contrasting color top, 1950s. **$25-$28**

Salt and Pepper Shakers, styrene plastic with diamond design, 1950s, unmarked. **$15-$18**

Salt and Pepper Shakers, styrene plastic with stylized vase and rose designs, 1950s, unmarked. **$15-$18**

Pop Up Toaster Salt and Pepper Set,
styrene plastic, bread slice shakers with toaster
holder, boxed, 1950s, a Starke design. **$22-$25**

**Miniature Mixer Salt and Pepper
Set,** styrene plastic with detachable
bowl for sugar, boxed 1950s. **$25-$28**

Serv-Rite Range Set Salt and Pepper Shakers, styrene plastic with contrasting lid, boxed, 1950s. **$12-$15**

Bean Pot Salt and Pepper Set, styrene plastic, boxed, 1950s, "It's a honey," Bee Plastics Inc., Cambridge, MA. **$18-$20**

Round Salt and Pepper Shakers, solid and clear styrene plastic, with flat bottoms, "Ideal for home, picnics, and seashore, Every smart hostess will use them," boxed, 1950s, Jiggs/Penny. **$15-$18**

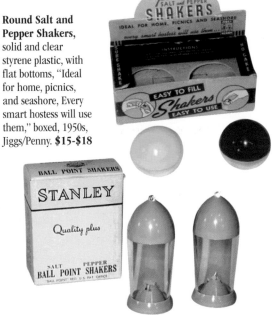

Stanley Ball Point Salt and Pepper Shakers, clear and solid styrene plastic with missile-shaped design, boxed, 1950s, Stanley Home Products Co. **$12-$15**

Serv-Rite Corn Salt and Pepper Shakers, two styrene plastic sets, boxed, 1950s, Royal Pacific Co., Los Angeles, CA. **$15-$18**

Steri-lite Tongs and Shakers Set, styrene plastic, 1950s. **$30-$35**

Chapter 23

Serving Dishes, Lazy Susans

Consumers eagerly took to the advantages of plastic serving dishes in the 1950s. Lighter in weight and more break resistant than their glass counterparts, they were also much lower in cost. Plastic dishes were easily transformed into a multitude of brightly colored shapes and styles, varying from simple bowls to exotic tropical and lotus leaf shapes. Some companies offered novel features like flip-top lids, finger holes, and multiple-piece sets with serving utensils. Of most interest to collectors today are sets with an original box having fun graphics. Any unusual shapes or features add to their appeal.

Lazy susans offer a simple, compact way of serving a selection of items. Popular with snacks, candies, or vegetables one server eliminates the need for a number of separate ones. Most rotate, hence the term "lazy," offering additional convenience and ease for the user. Plastic versions in the 1950s were lighter and easier to carry than comparable glass and wood units and are usually smaller in size. Many varieties exist and are usually harder to find than those made of other materials, since they couldn't withstand as much repeated use. Special features such as unusual colors or lids add to collector appeal.

Deluxe Serving Tray, styrene plastic, large size in two-tone yellow and green with brown center, 1950s, Another Superlon Product, Superior Plastics, Chicago, IL. **$25-$28**

Saturday Evening Post, November 11, 1961, with cover illustration by George Hughes. The serving line of a fancy dinner party is being invaded by a member of the younger set. The lady behind the table, obviously his mom, is doing her dignified best to ignore him. **$8-$10**

Lazy Susan, styrene plastic, angular-shaped design in two-tone yellow and green, 1950s, Beacon Plastics. **$18-$22**

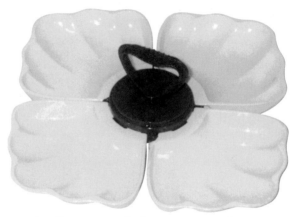

Lazy Susan, styrene plastic, two-tone green and
yellow, 1950s, Federal Tool Corp., Chicago, IL. **$15-$18**

Hi-Snack Plates, set of four, styrene plastic, "The plate that holds both glass and snacks in one hand, No juggling," boxed, 1950s, A Serv-Rite Product, Alexander & Wilson Co., Pasadena, CA. **$22-$25**

Deluxe Lazy Susan, large size in two-tone green and yellow with clear section covers, 1950s, Federal Tool Corp., Chicago, IL. **$28-$35**

Tele-Servers, styrene plastic, set of four,
server and tumbler sets, "For TV serving,
handy, convenient," boxed, 1950s, APCO,
Associated Plastic Corp., Chicago, IL. **$25-$28**

Coaster/Snack Dish, styrene plastic, set of three, 1950s, Federal Tool Corp., Chicago, IL. **$8-$10**

Tropical Moon Coasters, set of eight, styrene plastic, "Not an ashtray," boxed, 1950s, Hoffman Industries Inc., Sinking Springs, PA. **$20-$22**

Serving Set, large bowl with eight small bowls, styrene plastic, 1950s, Burrite, The Burroughs Co., Los Angeles, CA. **$22-$25**

Salad Set, styrene plastic, nine-piece set with flower design, 1950s, Hoffman Industries Inc., Sinking Springs, PA. **$22-$25**

Lanai Salad Set, deluxe six pieces, styrene plastic with serving tongs, boxed, 1950s, Flex "BW" Ware. **$25-$28**

Met-l-tone Salad Festival, seven pieces, styrene plastic, service for four, "Colorful with any interior," boxed, 1950s, Sterling Plastics, Union, NJ. **$25-$28**

California Fiesta Serving Set, six pieces, styrene plastic with serving tongs, "Ideal for salads, chips, popcorn, etc.," boxed, 1950s. **$28-$30**

Snack-Set, five pieces, melamine plastic, "For popcorn, salad, potato chips," with packaging card, 1960s-1970s, United Plastic Co., Townsend, MA. **$15-$18**

Leaf Server, styrene plastic with metal carrying handle and utensils, 1950s, A Karoff Original. **$18-$20**

Traymaster Deluxe Server, clear styrene plastic
with metallic retractable lids, 1950s. **$22-$25**

Chapter 24

Strainers, Presses, Etc.

Strainers are a kitchen aid to process or liquefy solid foods. They are also used to make applesauce, purees, etc. They vary in complexity from simple handheld wire mesh units, to versions with a separate mashing element or mechanical plunger action. Presses for hamburgers aided in forming convenient, uniform patties that could be frozen for later use. Strainers and presses vary from early primitive models to those of more recent manufacture. Unusual examples, and those having colorful original packaging, are of most interest to collectors.

Aldon Products ad from *House Furnishing Review,* July 10, 1948.

Metal Ricer and Press, with stand and wood wedging element, 1930s-1940s. **$15-$18**

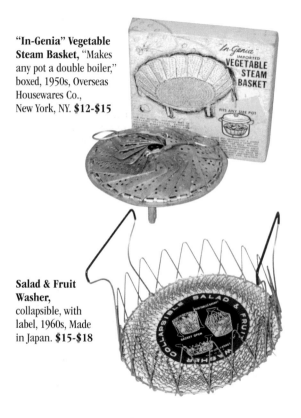

"In-Genia" Vegetable Steam Basket, "Makes any pot a double boiler," boxed, 1950s, Overseas Housewares Co., New York, NY. **$12-$15**

Salad & Fruit Washer, collapsible, with label, 1960s, Made in Japan. **$15-$18**

Handy Fruit Press & Potato Ricer, with sleeve, 1950s, Handy Things Mfg. Co., Ludington, MI. **$22-$25**

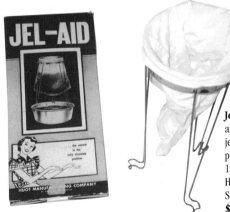

Jel-Aid, "The answer to the jelly straining problem," boxed, 1940s-1950s, Huot Mfg. Co., St. Paul, MN. **$18-$22**

SteaMarvel Steamer, metal, "Safe and sanitary, saves vitamins," boxed, 1960s-1970s, Aero Industrial Co., Burbank, CA. **$10-$12**

Ricer or Juicer, cast metal, 1930s, large **$18-$22;** small **$12-$15**

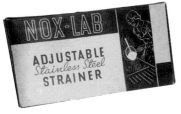

"Nox-Lab," adjustable strainer, stainless steel, boxed, 1930s, Knox Laboratories, Knox, IN. **$18-$20**

"Slice-a-Slice" Bread Slicer, metal apparatus holds a bread slice in place, so it can be sliced again for thin party sandwiches, canapés, etc. Boxed, 1940s-1950s deluxe set with knife, Aldon Products Co., Duncannon, PA. **$20-$22**

"Chef" Hamburger Patty Press, aluminum, "Quick, easy, sanitary," boxed, 1950s, Chef Products Co., Elkhart, IN. **$20-$25**

"Slice-a-Slice" Bread Slicer, boxed unit alone. **$15-$18**

Deluxe Hamburger Press, chrome plated, "For kitchen, patio, and barbecue use," boxed, 1950s, Kitchen Quip Inc., Waterloo, IN. **$12-$15**

Jumbo Hamburger Press, wood with
painted rooster design, boxed, 1950s, Western
Woods Inc., Portland, OR. **$22-$25**

"Form 'N Fry" Hamburger Press,
aluminum plunger action, "Easy to use,
Saves time too," boxed, 1950s, David Douglas
& Co. Inc., Manitowoc, WI. **$12-$15**

**Villaware Juicer/
Strainer Set,**
polypropylene, two-
piece juicer with
bowl, in package,
1960s-1970s. **$8-$10**

Chapter 25

Thermometers

Thermometers are another basic kitchen aid with numerous versions produced over the years. The major types include roast meat models having a metal prong to insert into the meat, and glass-enclosed candy or jelly thermometers for inserting into a hot liquid. Other varieties, such as freestanding models for oven use or barbecue grill thermometers, were also made. Vintage thermometers were originally sold separately or in sets. Basic sets would typically include meat and candy thermometers and deluxe sets added basters, skewers, wall racks, etc. Boxed thermometers have the most appeal to collectors today, with colorful box graphics or special features adding interest.

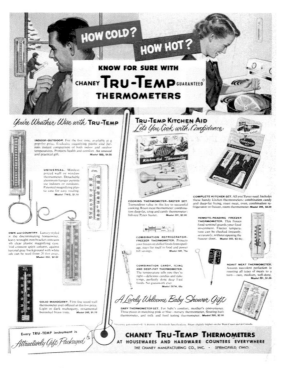

"Tru-Temp" Thermometers ad from
Life Magazine, November 22, 1954.

"Thermometers for the culinary art," deluxe set with thermometers, baster, measuring spoons, skewers. boxed, 1950s, Thermometer Corp. of America, Springfield, OH. **$25-$28**

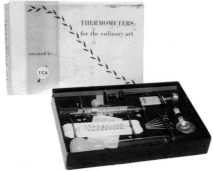

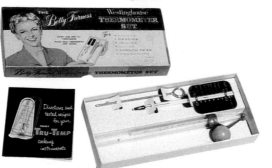

The Betty Furness Westinghouse Thermometer Set, for roasts, candies, deep fat, etc., boxed, 1950s, Cheney Mfg. Co., Springfield, OH. **$18-$22**

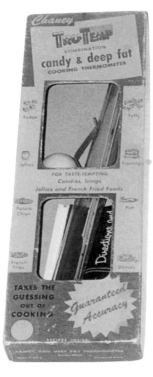

"Tru-Temp" Candy & Deep Fat Cooking Thermometers, "Takes the guesswork out of cooking," boxed, 1950s, Chaney Mfg. Co. **$10-$12**

Kitchen Aid Cooking Set, with handy protective wall bracket, boxed, 1950s-1960s, Chaney Tru-Temp Div. of Thermometer Corp. of America, Springfield, OH. **$15-$18**

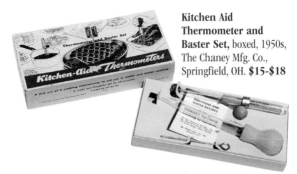

Kitchen Aid Thermometer and Baster Set, boxed, 1950s, The Chaney Mfg. Co., Springfield, OH. **$15-$18**

Chef-Master Cooking Thermometer, boxed, 1950s, W.C. Dillon & Co., Chicago, IL. **$12-$15**

Ohio Cooking Set, deep fat and meat thermometers, "Measure the degree of your cooking success," boxed, 1950s, Ohio Thermometer Co., Springfield, OH. **$12-$15**

Taylor Candy, Jelly, & Deep Frying Thermometer, boxed, 1950s, Taylor Instrument Co., Rochester, NY. **$10-$12**

Sears Candy, Jelly, Fat Thermometer, in cardboard tube, 1960s, sold by Sears Roebuck & Co. **$10-$12**

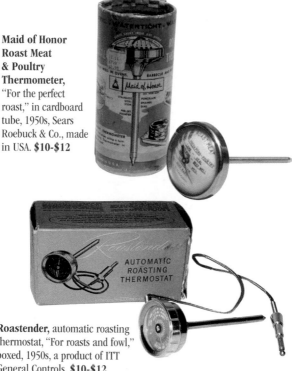

**Maid of Honor
Roast Meat
& Poultry
Thermometer,**
"For the perfect
roast," in cardboard
tube, 1950s, Sears
Roebuck & Co., made
in USA. **$10-$12**

Roastender, automatic roasting
thermostat, "For roasts and fowl,"
boxed, 1950s, a product of ITT
General Controls. **$10-$12**

Cooper Broil-Well Thermometer, "For all
outdoor cooking," on card, 1950s, Cooper
Thermometer Co., Pequabuck, CT. **$10-$12**

Meat Thermometer, "No more guesswork," on card, 1950s, Elpo Industries Inc., New York, NY. **$10-$12**

Taylor Oven Guide, metal, free-standing unit for oven use, boxed, 1950s, Taylor Instrument Co. **$12-$15**

Taylor Candy, Jelly, and Frosting Thermometer, metal and plastic. boxed, 1950s, Taylor Instrument Co. **$12-$15**

Chapter 26

Tupperware

In 1938, Earl S. Tupper began custom molding plastic items in Farnumsville, Mass. By 1945, he produced his first polyethylene product, a seven ounce juice tumbler. At the time, polyethylene was a recently developed plastic compound with never-before-seen features. It was flexible, durable, opalescent, and suitable for many types of applications.

For consumers, polyethylene was truly a novelty and as its qualities became known, its acceptance grew. This early phase culminated in a full-color feature about Tupperware in the October 1947 issue of *House Beautiful* titled "Fine Art for 39 cents." This boost in awareness helped Earl Tupper expand retail sales, as well as sales in his newly created home party plan division. Earl Tupper soon was promoting his products as being made of "Poly-T," not just ordinary polyethylene, and he also introduced pastel shades. By 1951, Tupperware Home Parties was formed to sell via dealers on the party plan, while retail sales were phased out. It turned out that some features of the product, including the exclusive Tupperware seal, could best be shown and sold through a person-to-person demonstration.

Through the 1950s, Tupperware continued its upward sales trend and additional items and manufacturing capacity were added. In 1956, the simplified elegance of Tupperware was given further acclaim when several containers were put on display in an exhibition at New York's Metropolitan Museum of Art. By 1958, the multimillion-dollar Tupperware operation was acquired by Rexall Drug & Chemical Co., later renamed Dart Industries.

Today, Tupperware is somewhat of a sleeper as a collectible. One drawback is difficulty in judging age and scarcity, as well as a seemingly endless supply of the product. Little vintage packaging or point-of-sale materials exist that would interest collectors, since many items were originally sold in a simple plastic bag or tied with a ribbon. Sets in pastel shades and early unusual items are attracting interest on the Internet; however, prices for the most part remain reasonable. It takes an appreciation of object simplicity, somewhat akin to admiring Shaker furniture, to appreciate Tupperware. However, with the retro allure of pastel shades and its simple functionality, new collectors continue to be attracted to Tupperware.

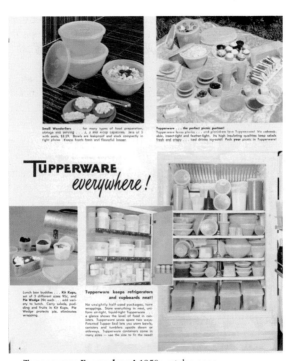

Tupperware Everywhere! 1950s catalog page demonstrates how Tupperware can keep your refrigerator and cupboards neat, and organize your next picnic.

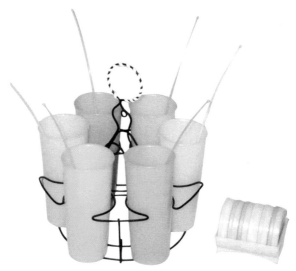

Tupperware Tumblers, six, 16 oz., in pastel shades with set of matching Tumbler Mates stirs, 1950s-1960s. **$22-$28;** Wire Caddy, not Tupperware, 1950s. **$15-$18;** Tupperware Wagon Wheel Coaster Set, six in pastel shades with handy Caddy, 1950s-1960s. **$12-$15**

Wonderlier Bowl Set, five sizes in pastel
shades with lids, 1950s-1960s. **$45-$50**

Tupperware Pitcher, 2 qt capacity, 1950s-1960s. Add **$3-$5** if lid is present. **$8-$10;** Tupperware Tumblers, six, 9 oz., in pastel shades, 1950s-1960s. **$18-$20**

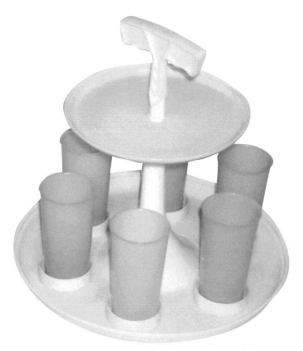

Tupperware Carousel Caddy, holds six tumblers and has tray for cookies or other food, 1960s. **$18-$22** without tumblers

Tupperware Salad Tongs, "Service-talented," boxed, 1950s-1960s. **$15-$18**

Tupperware Lazy Susan, 1950s, unmarked styrene plastic. **$15-$18**

Tupperware Tumblers, 2 oz. "Midgets" with seals, set of six in pastel shades, 1950s-1960s. **$12-$15;** Plastic Spice Rack, styrene plastic, non Tupperware, 1950s. **$12-$15**

Tupperware Grid Top Colander, colander base with open net lid, 1960s. **$12-$15**

Tupperware Colander, 1950s. **$12-$15**

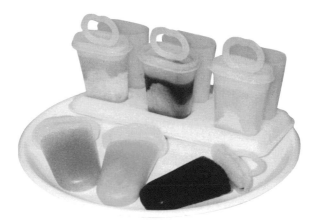

Tupperware Ice Tups Set, six molds with
handles and tray, 1950s-1960s. **$18-$20**

Bibliography

Arnold, Lionel K. *Introduction to Plastics.* Ames, IA: The Iowa State University Press, 1968.

Bercovici, Ellen; Bryson, Bobbie Zucker; Gillham, Deborah. *Collectibles for the Kitchen, Bath and Beyond.* Iola, WI: Krause Publications, 2001.

Celehar, Jane H. *Kitchens and Gadgets, 1920-1950.* Radnor, PA: Wallace-Homestead, 1982.

Cohn, Jan. *Covers of the Saturday Evening Post.* New York, NY: Smithmark Publishers, 1998.

Fenichell, Stephen. *Plastic, The Making of a Synthetic Century.* New York, NY: Harper Collins Publishers, Inc., 1996.

Franklin, Linda Campbell. *300 Years of Kitchen Collectibles.* Iola, WI: Krause Publications, 2001.

Goldberg, Michael J. *Collectible Plastic Kitchenware and Dinnerware.* Atglen, PA: Schiffer Publishing, Ltd., 1995.

Goldberg, Michael J. *Groovy Kitchen Designs for Collectors, 1935-1965.* Atglen, PA: Schiffer Publishing, Ltd., 1996.

Hine, Thomas. *Populuxe.* New York, NY: Borzoi Books, 1986.

Lifshey, Earl. *The Housewares Story.* Chicago, IL: The National Housewares Manufacturers Association, 1973.

Mantranga, Victoria Kasuba. *America at Home, A Cellibration of Twentieth-Century Housewares.* Rosemont, IL: The National Housewares Manufacturers Association, 1997.

Mauzy, Barbara E. *The Complete Book of Kitchen Collecting.* Atglen, PA: Schiffer Publishing, Ltd., 1997.

McDaniel, Patricia. *Drugstore Collectibles.* Radnor, PA: Wallace–Homestead, 1996.

Sparke, Penny. *The Plastics Age.* Woodstock, NY: The Overlook Press, 1993.

Stoneback, Diane. *Kitchen Collectibles, The Essential Buyer's Guide.* Radnor, PA: Wallace-Homestead, 1994.

Ward, Pete. *Fantastic Plastic, The Kitsch Collector's Guide.* Edison, NJ: Chartwell Books, 1997.

ITEM INDEX

About the Author

Brian S. Alexander was born in Peru, Indiana, and raised in Michigan City, Indiana. He studied Interdisciplinary Engineering at Purdue University where he invented and designed products in his spare time. This effort produced a patent for a baton twirling doll, a game, and a pet-rock-like novelty product, "Clothing for Telephones," that was featured in several newspaper articles.

He presently works in architecture and has homes in Evanston, Ill. and Michigan City, Ind.

Here I am trying out a 1950s comic barbecue apron.

A dedicated James Dean fan, with whom he shares a similar birthday and county origin, in the 1990s he set out to redecorate his home in the style of the 1950s. This exposed him to all types of gadgets and household items of the period. His interests as a collector took him to over 200 antique malls, shops, flea markets, and shows from Columbus, Ohio, to Des Moines, Iowa, and on more than a few Internet excursions. As his collections grew, he thought that someday he might write a book on the subject. In 2001, Eric Zorn at the *Chicago Tribune* started a motivational program where individuals start working on one of their long put-off "someday projects," and Brian signed up. After over two years of work, you are holding the results in your hands. Contact Brian at Spiffykitchen@hotmail.com.